D0763798

START YOUR NOVEL

SIX WINNING STEPS TOWARD A
COMPELLING OPENING LINE,
SCENE AND CHAPTER

DARCY PATTISON

MIMS HOUSE
LITTLE ROCK, ARKANSAS

Mims House
1309 S. Broadway
Little Rock, AR 72202
www.mimshouse.com

Book Layout ©2013 BookDesignTemplates.com

Ordering Information:
Quantity sales. Special discounts are available on quantity purchases by corporations, associations, and others. For details, contact the publisher at the address above.

Start Your Novel/Darcy Pattison —1st edition
ISBN 978-0-9852134-2-8

Contents

Other How-to-Write Books by Darcy Pattison
Novel Metamorphosis: UnCommon Ways to Revise
How to Write a Children's Picture Book
The Book Trailer Manual

Children's Books by Darcy Pattison
11 Ways to Ruin a Photograph
*Wisdom, the Midway Albatross: Surviving the Japanese Tsunami
and Other Disasters for over 60 Years*

Other Books by Darcy Pattison
*Common Core ELA Activities: Month by Month Writing, Speaking and
Listening Activities Aligned with the Common Core*

For more information, see
http://www.darcypattison.com/darcy-pattison-books/

[1]

Starting the Journey

YOU WANT TO WRITE A STORY OR A NOVEL, and you need to know how to begin. This book will help you generate ideas, choose the right opening scene, write a compelling first page and a killer first line. You'll apply examples, writing techniques, tips and strategies to write a great first draft of an opening scene or chapter. But that's not enough: I'll also suggest how to evaluate the draft, improve weak openings and make sure the opening sets up the ending.

OPENING CHAPTERS MUST ACCOMPLISH THESE GOALS

GRAB YOUR READER'S ATTENTION. Something must grab the reader's attention immediately. This can be an unusual use of language, a unique voice, a startling action, a dynamic bit of dialogue, an active description of setting, or a strange mood. Get attention fast. You may only have three or four seconds before the reader closes your book and reaches for the next one.

GROUND THE READER IN THE SETTING. The reader needs to know immediately WHEN and WHERE the story is taking place. Please use specifics here: Is this 1825 or 1977? Are we in Manitoba, Canada, one of the Florida Keys or on the Moon? Specific sensory details should cue the reader to the exact location, even if you don't specifically say where we are in the first couple paragraphs.

INTRIGUE THE READER WITH A CHARACTER. Even a reader who loves action-adventure is fascinated by a character's life. The biggest difference between films and novels is the novelist's ability to get inside the character's head. Films can only imply thoughts and motivations; novels can delve deeply into the inner life of a character. And the novel must open with a character who entices the reader to stay awhile and get acquainted.

GIVE THE READER A PUZZLE TO SOLVE. The plot, the events of the novel, should give the reader an immediate puzzle to solve, something to worry about, something to make him or her want to read on to find out what happens next. The puzzle must start on page one! Not page 3 and certainly not page 25. The reader must want to turn the page to find out what happens next.

SET THE PACE. Each novel demands a certain pace. One may start slow and build, while another may start with a bang. The reader should get a sense of that pace in the opening. A fast-pace action scene might signal a novel with break-neck speed. A slower paced opening might signal a leisurely character novel. The opening should set the pace so the reader knows what to expect.

YOUR WRITING PROCESS

One of the first issues you must deal with is the storytelling process. Among writers, one of the most passionate discussion hinges on whether to plan a story extensively (outliners), or write by-the-seat-of-your-pants (pantsters or organic writers), or take a middle route of some planning, but then letting the writing lead the story to unexpected places (plansters). I believe the issue is personal to each writer and their individual working methods. Outliners often create tighter first drafts and shortcut the revision process. Successful organic writers seem to have an inherent sense of story and conflict, and they instinctively reach for the next chapter or scene; they may go unusual directions but first drafts have a looser structure. Plansters have the advantage of early structure, but allow for diversions along the way; they still have to come back and organize later, though. Whichever way you choose, engaging stories can result.

For organic writers, this book will ask you to plan beyond your comfort level. For outliners, you may think the planning is too truncated. Whatever your personal writing process, engaging writing can result. And here, we'll focus on examining fully the issues that determine if you can execute the vision of your story.

[2]

Why Editors Focus on Page 1

AN EDITOR CAN TELL within a couple of pages if a manuscript will work for their publishing house. How? What is it that makes this decision so clear to an editor and so muddy to an author?

The first pages of a novel encapsulate so much of the story and are extremely important to establish setting, character, pace, audience, tone, voice and more. First pages give readers a doorknob to turn, an opening to the whole story. Editors are sophisticated, critical readers and a slight misstep in the opening may cause them to put down the story and never pick it up again.

AUDIENCE. Sometimes, the discussion about a first page centers on the intended audience. This means the actual writing will appeal to a certain audience and not to others. Age level (picture book, early reader, early chapter, tween, middle grade, young adult or teen, new adult, or adult), genre (historical fiction, science fiction and fantasy, mystery, contemporary, etc.), and trade v. education markets are easy to separate out from a couple of opening lines. Editors look to see if the author has slanted the storytelling for a certain audience.

TOO LITTLE INFORMATION. Some pages leave the reader and editor alike confused. Where are we and what is going on? Perhaps the author tried to create a sense of mystery, but in the process held back too much information. Or the story has a naive narrator, but that point-of-view leaves the editor with too little information. This type of misstep means the editor puts down the book because they just don't understand what is happening, or the importance of what is happening.

TOO MUCH INFORMATION. On the other end of the spectrum is the possibility of too much backstory, description, flashbacks, or facts. This type of information dump probably slows the pacing and includes too much, well, boring stuff. An editor only needs enough to understand the scene-in-progress. Editors can edit out the information dump, but they worry that inappropriate exposition in the first pages might carry over in the writing style and organization throughout the book.

NO OPENING SCENE. Some manuscripts open with description, interior thoughts of characters, or first-person musings that continue for the whole first chapter. The opening scene is missing. These manuscripts tend to lose an editor's attention because nothing is happening. The editor is bored.

SUCCESSFUL BALANCE. Successful manuscripts are well balanced, starting with an active protagonist involved in a scene with an immediate, concrete goal. They are balanced with action, thought, a touch of motivation, a touch of description. The tone and voice are interesting and editors will want to turn the page to see what happens next.

Here's an opening from the Prologue of the memoir *Breaking Night* by Liz Murray. It's the actual opening of the book.

> *I have just one picture left of my mother. It's 4 x 7, black-and-white, and creased in different places. In it, she is seated slightly hunched, elbows touching knees, arms carrying the weight of her back. I know very little about her life when it was taken; my only clue is written in orange marker on the back. It reads: Me in front of Mike's on 6th St. 1971. Counting backward, I know that she was seventeen when it was taken, a year older than I am now. I know that Sixth Street is in Greenwich Village, though I have no idea who Mike is.*
>
> *--Prologue of Breaking Night by Liz Murray, Hyperion, c. 2010.*

What do you know about the story from just this much text?

    Place: New York City

    Time: 1986

    Tone/Mood: Reflective, remembering, possibly nostalgic.

    First-person. POV narrator: 16-years-old, assumed to be
          female

    Content of text: It's about a black and white picture of the
          narrator's mother.

    Mystery: Who is Mike? Why is there only one picture of her
          mother left?

    Audience: Young Adult/Teen to Adults

Is there any place where the reader is confused? No, it's clear.

Is there an information dump? There is a lot of information here, but it doesn't feel like a dump, yet, because we are also getting a feel for the character of the story. That gives the author some leeway to put in lots of information, while still keeping everything balanced.

A FINAL QUESTION IS SUBJECTIVE: WOULD YOU READ ON? Even when you've done everything right, an editor may pass on a story because they just didn't like it. I once had an editor pass on a story about dogs because she's a cat person, not a dog person. There's nothing you can do about that except write the best you know how and then look for an editor who matches your passions.

[3]

STEP ONE: Clarify Your Idea

YOU HAVE AN IDEA FOR A STORY. NOW WHAT? The story needs clarity and development before you can ever start to write. A first draft is much like putting together a jigsaw puzzle. Except there's no box top to look at when writing a novel. There's only the vision in your mind for what the story could be.

To start developing your idea, look at the overall plot structure and think about where the story might go. First, create a list of possible scenes.

Let's take the case of Cinderella. What are the possible scenes for this story?

- Cinderella's mother and father meet.
- Cinderella's mother and father fall in love and marry.
- Cinderella's mother and father have a romantic night and she conceives.
- Cinderella is born and her mother dies in childbirth.
- Father meets a new woman and woos her.
- Father marries new woman.
- Stepmother and stepsisters move in.
- Stepmother and stepsisters are cruel.

- King declares a ball.
- Step-family says Cinderella can't go to the ball.
- After step-family leaves for the ball, Cinderella meets her fairy godmother who transforms her.
- Cinderella attends the ball and falls in love with Prince.
- Cinderella flees the ball and leaves behind her shoe.
- Prince seeks woman who can wear the shoe.
- Prince finds Cinderella; they get married and live happily ever after.

Notice that each of these could be fully developed into a complete scene or a set of scenes. When the King declares a ball, the scene might be set in his throne room, with courtiers present. Conflict could lie in the King's and Queen's relationship, the King's and Prince's relationship, or any variety of problems with courtiers.

Also notice that I've left out many, many possible scenes and some of these listed would take several scenes to fully develop. Partly that's because a simple list like this isn't sufficient; instead, you need to focus the scene list in some way. That means you need to know something about the type of story you want to write. Is this a story of rivalry or revenge, of rescue or about an underdog? Deciding on the type of story you want to write will help you focus your scene list. For that, let's review a series of plot templates and try out a couple for your story.

Plot Tutorials: 29 Plot Templates

Plot templates are helpful in telling an author the possible events for different sections of a story. The template slants the story in certain directions and implies certain events for Act 1, 2 or 3. In this early phase of story planning, it's helpful to know what is possible or typical for different types of stories. I consult the plot templates when I'm first thinking of an idea for a novel and again when I start a revision. Don't think that templates will dictate your story for you, though.

They are just a way of understanding the types of stories possible; you will want to create a unique variation that will hold a reader's interest.

As you read through each plot template think about what might happen in each act for such a story. Act 1 will always introduce the story problem and Act 3 will usually show resolution, either success or failure. Act 2 develops the story problem in unique ways. After you read through these, I'll use the Cinderella story as an example for how you might use the templates to help focus your own story.

THE TWO MOST SIMPLISTIC TEMPLATES

1. Adventure comes to you. A Stranger comes to town.

2. You go to Adventure. You leave town.

20 MORE PLOT TEMPLATES

In a more complex approach to plot templates, Ronald B. Tobias' book *20 Master Plots* discusses and suggests that almost all the stories in the world would fall into one of these categories.

3. Quest. A character oriented story, in which the protagonist searches for something and winds up changing him/herself.

4. Adventure. Focused on plot instead of character, this features a goal-oriented series of exciting events.

5. Pursuit. This is the typical Chase Plot, definitely action-oriented with Character A chasing Character B.

6. Rescue. This is another easy to recognize action-oriented plot, with Character A rescuing Character B.

7. Escape. For a variation on the Rescue, use this plot template when the protagonist escapes on his/her own.

8. Revenge. Ah, character comes back in with this one: someone is wronged and vows to take revenge on someone else.

9. The Riddle. Love a good mystery? This is the plot for you. It is simply a question that must be answered.

10. Rivalry. Character oriented, this story follows two main characters, one on a downward track and one on an upward track, along with their interactions.

11. Underdog. Everyone is the U.S. cheers for the Underdog. This is the plot where the under-privileged (handicapped, poor, etc.) character triumphs despite overwhelming odds.

12. Temptation. Here is Pandora's Box extended to novel form.

13. Metamorphosis. This plot involves a physical transformation of some kind. If you recently watched the movie "District 9," you'll recognize this plot form. It's *Dr. Jekyll and Mr. Hyde*, or *Beauty and the Beast*.

14. Transformation. Similar to the previous plot template, this plot features an inner change, instead of changing the outer form.

15. Maturation. Bildungsroman, rite of passage, coming-of-age— these terms all refer to someone growing up morally, spiritually or emotionally. Often, it's just a hint of growth, or a tiny change that hints at larger changes.

16. Love. Here's the classic Boy-meets-Girl plot. Boy Meets Girl. Boy and Girl hate each other. Boy gets Girl.

17. Forbidden Love. Oh, hasn't Stephenie Meyer milked this one in her *Twilight* series? It's a brilliant use of the forces that keep her characters apart, while still causing attraction. It's Romeo and Juliet.

18. Sacrifice. From the Biblical tale of Jesus to the story of parents sacrificing for their children, this is a staple of literature. Character A gives up something either because of a relationship with another character or for some moral reason.

19. Discovery. You know those secrets you've buried deep in your past? This story excavates and exposes such secrets and watches them affect the characters. Character A discovers X and suddenly the

world is different. This can be about the process of discovery, or it can incorporate the results of the discovery.

20. Wretched Excess. When a character is in a downward spiral from alcohol, drugs, greed, etc. this is the plot form. Character A starts in a lofty position, but ends the story in a lower position.

21 and 22. Ascension or Descension. A rise or fall from power puts a character into this plot form.

THE HERO'S JOURNEY PLOT

23. Then, there's the classic Hero's Journey, adapted from Joseph Campbell's Mythic Hero. Christopher Vogler's explanation of the Hero's Journey in his book, *The Writer's Journey*, is an excellent, detailed discussion of the basic stages of the journey, along with the corresponding character arc:

- Ordinary World – limited awareness of problem
- Call to Adventure – increased awareness
- Refusal of Call – reluctance to change
- Meeting the Mentor – overcoming reluctance
- Crossing the First Threshold – committing to change
- Tests, Allies, Enemies – experimenting with 1st change
- Approach to the Inmost Cave- preparing for big change
- Supreme Ordeal – attempting big change
- Reward – consequences of the attempt
- The Road Back – rededication to change
- Resurrection – final attempt at big change
- Return with Elixir – final mastery of the problem

24. You write comedy or humor and want a plot for a novel? John Vorhaus, in *The Comic Toolbox*, adapts the Hero's Journey into a Comic Throughline.

TWO CHARACTERS INTERACTING PLOT

25. Similar to the Hero's Journey is Peter Dunne's adaptation to a story in which two main characters influence each other, or one character drastically changes a second. *The Emotional Structure* details how the characters interact. Using the earlier templates, this could be a Rivalry story, a Love story, a Forbidden Love story, or even one of Pursuit, Rescue, or Escape. The emphasis here is that two characters act upon each other.

CARD'S MICE QUOTIENT PLOT

Taking a completely different tack, Orson Scott Card in his book, *Characters and Viewpoint*, asks in what aspect of the story are you most interested? One strength of this approach is that it tells you where to start and end your story. MICE=Milieu, Idea, Character, Event.

26. Milieu. When the setting is in the forefront, as it is in many science fiction and fantasy (sff) stories, you have a milieu story. The setting, culture, or world created is the focus of the story. This explains why Tolkein didn't stop *The Lord of the Rings* when the battle against Mordor was won; because the focus is on the milieu, he continues on, following the hobbits home, the leaving of the elves and so on, until the Age of Men is established.

27. Idea. A question is posed and answered. This is the classic mystery plot or the Riddle Plot as explained in previous templates.

28. Character. This story begins and ends with pure character and could be any of the character plots as explained in previous templates.

29. Event. Here, Card says that something in the universe is out of balance and the protagonist must right-the-wrong, restore-the-rightful-king, restore justice, defeat evil, etc. If *The Lord of the Rings* had been this type story, it would have indeed ended when the evil was defeated.

Are there more plot templates? Probably, but not many. Stories usually follow a template, not like they would a formula, but as a deep structure that we recognize as story. Narratives and narrative structure are engrained in the human psyche. (See Kendall Haven's interesting book, *Story Proof: The Science Behind the Startling Power of Story*.)

From these examples, you can see both the usefulness and limitations of using a template. You don't want a cookie-cutter plot; however, you need to meet the expectations of readers in a certain genre. Each type of story has typical actions and emotions for each stage of that story. When beginning your novel, using a template is an easy way to start exploring your story. Don't worry, there's time for originality later in the details of the story and in how you tell it.

USE PLOT TEMPLATES TO FOCUS THE STORY

Looking back at the 29 plot templates you could make a case for using many of them for Cinderella. Notice that each template would send the story off in a unique direction.

QUEST: Cinderella is on a quest, seeking a better place in life and finds that she must set aside appearances to see the inner character of people. This focuses more on her overall position in society.

RESCUE: From the Prince's point-of-view (POV), he must rescue Cinderella from the clutches of her evil stepmother. Here, the Prince's motivation is to save Cinderella, not necessarily to love her. Or, from Cinderella's POV, she wants to save her father from an evil woman.

REVENGE: The story could focus on how Cinderella takes revenge on her stepfamily. It's not a story that is often told but it's an interesting possibility.

RIVALRY: In the usual Cinderella story, the stepsisters are ugly and not real competition to the lovely Cinderella. But what if (and great stories are made from what ifs!) one of the stepsisters is a real rival. It's a new twist on the story.

UNDERDOG: Of course, the classic Cinderella story is about an underdog.

LOVE: Or is her story the classic love story? Girl meets Boy. Girl and Boy are kept apart by their different social statuses. Girl gets Boy.

ASCENSION: One option is to tell the story of Cinderella's rise to power in the kingdom. And what that power ultimately does to her. We would see her as powerless in Act 1, but by the beginning of Act 2, she has become princess and struggles with her new position. Act 3 tells the result of her struggles, either success or failure.

Each plot pattern would require a different set of scenes, emotions, motivations. Let's take the unusual one of Rivalry, just for fun.

CINDERELLA USING A RIVALRY PLOT

Once you decide on a particular plot template, it will help you focus your story. First, recognize the minimum requirements and optional features for your chosen plot template.

Characters: Cinderella, Prince, Beautiful Step-Sister (Optional: fairy godmother, father, stepmother, another stepsister, king, queen, servants, courtiers.)

Plot:

1. Girl meets boy.
2. Girl recognizes her rival in her Beautiful Step-Sister (BSS)
3. Girl attends series of events (Optional: a series of balls) in which she competes with BSS; a typical plot would have her fail most of these.
4. Girl has a final showdown with BSS for Prince's attention; some character quality, previously dismissed as unimportant will give her the victory; OR, Girl has final showdown with BSS for Prince's attention and loses (this would be the tragic version of the story). (Optional: a last ball.)
5. Girl gets boy (Tragic version: Girl does not get boy.)

Now is when you need to go back and think about events, settings, and actions that are implied by your plot template: some back story about Cinderella's position, a fairy godmother, a stepfamily (cruelness is optional, as long as you explain the cinders in her name), the presence of the father is optional, a kingdom with a prince, the optional king and queen, an event where the Prince meets the girls (traditionally a ball or dance, but that's optional), etc. It's time to start filling in the life and times of your characters.

You still have many decisions to make about tone, mood, the ending, which characters to include/exclude and more. Before you start writing, though, let's turn our attention to your character's pain.

Where Does Your Protagonist Hurt?

A second way to focus the story before you start writing is to develop the character and his/her emotional arc. How arc the plot events affecting the protagonist and where is s/he on the emotional arc of the story?

Characters must change and grow over the course of a story. Now is the time to decide what character quality you will focus on: Unfaithful to Loyal, Fearful to Confident, Unfair to Fair. The possibilities are infinite, but within the context of your focused plot decisions, the options narrow.

Cinderella as Rivalry:

- Vain to Indifferent (modest, shy, humble, unconceited)
- Jealous to Content
- Self-centered to Self-sacrifice
- Apathetic to Passionate

Here's the hard part: usually, you'll put the worst character trait first and your character will move toward becoming a better human. This means that your character starts out deeply flawed. As authors, we resist this starting position because we want characters that are likable and fun to write about. But those characters are boring. You must give the reader a character that has problems, hence conflicts, that can sustain a story over the long haul. Start with a character in trouble and you're halfway there. What character quality will challenge your protagonist?

The Biggest, Deepest Pain

A final thing to plan for is the protagonist's biggest and deepest pain. What is the character most afraid of; what could make the character hurt the most? Of course, you must make your character face that very thing. This painful event usually comes late in the 2nd act and can send the character into the 3rd act, or sometimes it happens somewhere in the 3rd act. If you use the Hero's Journey plot template, this is the Supreme Ordeal.

Why do you want to hurt your character? Remember, without conflict, there is no story. And you want a memorable story, something that moves the reader emotionally. That means you have to reach for the deepest emotions possible, which means you must hurt your character deeply (and thus touch your readers deeply).

I repeat: What scares your character the most? What would s/he never do? What would put more emotional pain at risk? You must make the character walk into that situation and face that pain.

Back to Cinderella: in the traditional Cinderella, she most fears appearing before the Prince as her cinder-covered-self. But he sees through the surface to the inner beauty.

In our story of Cinderella-as-Rivalry, we looked at character traits that make sense within the context of the Rivalry plot. Let's choose the Jealousy to Contentment arc and see how it plays out. Notice that the characters are getting names and starting to take on a personality, starting to become real to me as a writer.

Plot + Character Arc:

1. Cinderella meets the Prince Phillipe and falls in love and he seems to love her, too.

2. But then, Phillipe meets and is attracted to the Beautiful Step-Sister (let's name her Belinda) and jealousy overwhelms Cinderella.

3. Cinderella and Belinda attend several of the Phillipe's balls. Each time, Belinda insists that Cinderella wear the best gown, which endears her to Cinderella. As Cinderella fails again and again to gain Phillipe's attention, she is more and more jealous of Belinda. She refuses to admit that Belinda and Phillipe are good together.

4. At the last ball, Phillipe dances with the dazzling Cinderella, but then turns to Belinda and asks her to marry him. BIGGEST FEAR: Cinderella has lost the chance to marry the Prince and become a Princess.

5. Belinda gets Phillipe; Cinderella does not get Phillipe, however, it's OK with her because she has learned to love her stepsister and the sisterly love wins out in the end and she is genuinely happy for Belinda. Besides, the prince's bodyguard is pretty hot! She is content.

BECAUSE. One of the most important parts of this synopsis is the "because" statement in the last section. Even at this early stage of planning, it helps to know WHY the character changes, what emotional trigger has set up and caused the change. Here, it's because Cinderella has grown up as an only child and Belinda is such a nice sister.

When you do this sort of planning, it's important to recognize what has happened to the story, to understand where the development has taken it. Here, the character arc has moved the story away from a boy-girl love story; now it's ABOUT the stepsister's relationships because that is what dictates the happiness in the end. Cinderella and Belinda have the power to hurt each other the most in how they deal honestly and openly with the rivalry. Why does Cinderella feel contentment at the end? Because she has learned to love her stepsister and wants what is best for her. We only learn this true focus of the story as we follow through the character arc. That's why it is important to plan ahead; so right from the start, the story focuses on the sister's relationship. It's also easier at this early stage to shape an interesting twist on the Cinderella story; it resulted from early plot development, and likely, it would have been difficult to carry through without the planning.

REVISION IS SIMPLE AT THIS STAGE

What if you decide you don't want to write a story about how stepsisters relate? Great. You haven't spent too much time working on this story yet, so change it. Keep the Rivalry plot, but give her a different emotional arc. Adjust the plot template and emotional arc until you are satisfied it is a story that you can tell in a compelling way.

Having discovered the true theme of the story, you can delve even deeper into the character's pains and deepen the story further.

PLANNING WITH PLOT + CHARACTER

Once you know more about your basic plot and your characters, it's time to really get to work. From here, it's always a messy matter for me to develop the story because I go back and forth between character and plot and the implied events from the plot template. The focus gleaned from using the plot template and the character work makes it easier.

One way of moving on is to refine the list of possible scenes. Given these characters and a basic plot template, what scenes could take place? What should take place? What must take place? Your answer will differ from mine, and that's as it should be.

If our Cinderella story is about the stepsister's relationship, then what are possible conflicts, how can the stepsisters clash? The stepsisters must share a bedroom, work together, care for each other when sick, plan for each other's birthday (Hey! Maybe they were born on the same day.), sew ball gowns for each other and so on. Notice that when you're in the midst of this, other ideas might occur, such as the same-day-birthdays. Take all these plot or character developments as gifts and work with them, weeding out what doesn't work and fertilizing what does. Certainly, the opening scene must be between the sisters; the father and stepmother are secondary to the story, so they probably won't be in the opening scene, just the girls. Through it all, look for something unusual, original, fresh.

In other words, you are still trying to figure out who, what, when, where, and why--the basics of a good story and scene. Take time to think through the implications of each element. If character A is buying coffee, what does that tell about him: his age, access to cash, location, passions, etc.? At this stage, think deeply about the implications of each decision. If the stepsisters share a birthday, what does that mean for the birthday celebration, type of presents, etc.? Will their birthday fall on same day as a royal ball? Even if Belinda likes Cinderella, does the stepmother like Cinderella? And so on.

Keep in Mind as you Work on Plot+Character

CONFLICT ON EVERY PAGE: What conflict is possible in a castle? What would be a funny conflict, a sad conflict, an enraging conflict, etc.? Is each event truly worthy of a full scene?

CAUSE-EFFECT RELATIONSHIPS: You need to see connections from one scene to the next. What will carry over from one to the next in a direct or indirect way?

BUILDING TOWARD END OF ACT I: The end of Act I is a small climax that sends our characters and plot into the fray with commitment and a sense that they can't back out, the only way out now is to go forward into Act 2. How can you foreshadow, build in progressions, connect scenes, etc. in such a way that there is a high point at the end of Act 1? It starts on page one.

DON'T GIVE AWAY TOO MUCH: While you want to foreshadow, to prepare the audience for any plot twists later, it needs to be subtle.

NO BACK STORY: In Act 1, you will NOT stop and give any backstory! If you feel compelled to write something about that, you will write it, but hold it in reserve for much later in the story when it can have an emotional impact. Some people suggest chapter two is the backstory; however, Donald Maass, in *Writing the Breakout Novel*, suggests waiting until page 100 for a flashback, or significant backstory. Keep the Act I grounded in the present time and in the present scene. When you must add backstory before page 100, keep it brief and keep it directly tied to the immediate scene. Act I must stay in the immediate action and progress without flashbacks. We'll discuss the issue of backstory and flashbacks in more detail in a later chapter.

TIMELINE: From scene to scene, what is the time jump? Can you tighten that in any way, or can you plan better scene cuts? How can you keep a tight pace?

START WITH A SCENE: Unless you are definitely writing a character novel, start with a scene. There's a beginning: a character goes into a situation with a goal. There's a middle: the character encounters conflict and doesn't get what s/he wants. There's an end: most scenes will end in a disaster and the character must find a new goal to send him/her into a new scene. If the character achieves his/her goal—then the story is over. No more conflict, no more story. You'll read more about writing in scenes in the next section.

You can expect to go round and round on the story in this early stage, trying one thing and then another. Expect to write a few sample scenes or so, trying out the voice, the setting, the character interactions, etc.

Expect everything to be messy for a while.

But in the end, one scene will rise above the others as the beginning of the story. Strong first chapters are essential to great novels. Revise and rethink and re-envision the starting point of your story until you find the best place to begin.

If you're an outliner, you will certainly want to get more specific at every level; if you are an organic writer, you're way past your comfort zone in planning a story structure and you are aching to get started. If you're a planster, you're likely right in your comfort zone with some things figured out, but not too much. But all types of story-planners need to hold off and first review some novel writing skills.

[4]

STEP TWO: Review Your Skills

TWO WRITING SKILLS ARE ESSENTIAL to creating a publishable manuscript: writing in scenes and writing with vivid imagery. A review of your skills here will ensure that you write a strong first draft.

What has the most potential for improving your writing? Learning to write a strong scene; then making sure every scene in your story is strong. It's not mandatory—there are good books written without strong scenes—but I find that beginning to intermediate writers are more likely to succeed with a strong scene structure.

A scene is a series of connected actions that contain a small story question. Will John get a home run in this game? The scene will focus on one baseball game and the question of John's prowess with a bat. Scenes are places where the author slows down the story and tells what happens blow-by-blow. It's a zoom, a close-up focus, which gives a reader an immersive experience, as if they are actually watching events unfold.

Scenes are the natural chunks of story and are connected with some narration (telling) to smooth the transitions from scene to scene. Strong scenes are the building blocks of great stories.

THE SCENE BOX TEST

Do you write in scenes or not? Try this.

Choose 2-3 chapters of a work-in-progress, print it out and then mark it this way: start by putting a box around each scene. It may cover several pages, or it may be very short. The scene structure may be loose and not fully developed, but within that box, there should be some sense of movement toward a goal.

NOTE TO SCREENWRITERS: If you're used to writing scripts, scenes in a novel work a little bit different. For scripts, scenes are mandatory and a new scene starts any time the location changes. For example, if a character is outside a house and walks inside, it's a scene change because the camera has to move. Scenes in scripts tend to be short. For a novel, a scene can extend longer and cover several minor changes of setting. So, if you're used to writing scripts, think instead of scene sequences, or a series of scenes that cover a distinct goal of a character.

If you're still fuzzy on scenes, just try drawing boxes and see what happens. We will be spending some time on writing scenes anyway, so this is just a sort of pre-check to see where you stand.

What did you find? Did you write in scenes? Or did the story actions stop abruptly, to be replaced with narrative fluff? If you are not writing in scenes, we will cover the basics here and you will see vast improvement.

If you did write in scenes, answer these questions:
- Does each scene have a series of actions?
- Is there a beginning, middle and end?
- Does the outcome of the scene make a difference in the story?

- Out of all the possibilities, why did you choose to write THIS scene in your novel? At this point in the story, why did you slow down and zoom in on details to SHOW-DON'T-TELL this particular scene?
- Is there an engine, a question, a pulse, a tension, an anticipation—something that runs through the scene and makes you want to turn the page?

ESSENTIAL WRITING SKILL #1: SCENE BASICS

Let's review the basics of a scene mentioned briefly earlier.

There's a beginning: A character goes into a situation with a goal. There's a middle: the character encounters conflict and doesn't get what s/he wants. There's an end: most scenes will end in a disaster and the character must find a new goal to send him/her into a new scene. If the character achieves his/her goal—then the story is over. No more conflict, no more story.

Scenes are created by actions and one easy way to make sure you have exciting actions slotted into the structure is to create a beat sheet. A beat sheet is a list of the actions of a scene.

Suppose we want to write about John's baseball game. What are possible beats of action?

- Dressing in team uniform
- Traveling to the game
- Arriving at game
- Warming up

Wait right there. These are all too general to be an effective beat sheet; also, some of these lack the conflict necessary for a good scene. Instead, a beat sheet is going to zoom into the action, slow down the time line and put the reader into the middle of the action and the conflict. Here's another try at a beat sheet for John.

- Grab glove from dugout bench (action that sets scene)
- Open gym bag in search of a ball (character: he's forgetful)

- Toss ball up and down (character: nervous about game)
- Accept a piece of bubble gum from Catcher (character: shows friendship)
- Throw away gum wrapper and chomp on gum (pure action)
- On the way to outfield, he stops to tie right shoelace (action that moves the story along, the game is about to start)
- Center Field runs by and says, hurry up (character: relationship with Center Field; potential conflict)
- Answer Center Field with a grunt (character: more on relationship with Center Field)
- Run to Left Field (action that moves the story along)

This beat sheet might be suitable for the beginning of a scene. It seems to lack conflict in the opening sections, though, so I would likely try again. Revising at this level is easier than revising fully developed text, so make it a practice to ask at every stage, "Where's the conflict?"

When writing the scene, you may only include a few of the beats, but the beauty of planning the small actions ahead is that you can choose which are the most important. Does John trip over his shoelaces later, bruising his shoulder, so he can't bat well? Or are the shoelaces just not important to the story? Whichever beats you finally use, they should be there for a reason: to set up something, to characterize, to set the scene, to develop the action, etc.

Also, over the course of the scene, the actions or beats need to develop the story, create tension (Center Field better say out of John's way!), and lead to a disaster at the end of the scene. Writing out the beats ahead of time means you can choose where to focus the scene and choose the best actions from those possible.

Finally, it's helpful to think about writing a scene that has a turning point or pivot point somewhere. That is, the scene is developing in one direction, but some beat or action turns everything around.

One of the easiest ways to see this is to watch the "Harvard Bar" scene from the popular movie, *Good Will Hunting*. Watch this video on YouTube: http://youtu.be/ymsHLkB8u3s (Rated PG13 for some language.) Watch it before you come back to these questions and discussion of scenes.

QUESTIONS:
- What happens in the beginning phase?
- What happens in the middle phase?
- What is the turning point or focal point of the scene?
- How does the scene end: in a disaster (tragedy), in success, or somewhere in between? At the end, what has changed for each character?
- What is the setting for this scene? Why is this an appropriate scene for the action that happens?
- What are the underlying emotions of the scene?
- If you know the larger story, list at least three reasons why this is a necessary scene for this story.
- What else do you notice about scenes by studying this film clip?

QUESTIONS WITH DISCUSSION:
- What happens in the beginning phase? The gang walks into a bar, and Chuckie sees a couple girls and decides to talk to them.
- What happens in the middle phase? Chuckie tries to pick up girls and is interrupted by a Harvard guy who tries to make fun of him.
- What is the turning point or focal point of the scene? Will steps in to defend Chuckie and put down the Harvard guy.
- How does the scene end: in a disaster (tragedy), in success, or somewhere in between? At the end, what has changed for

each character? Success: Will obviously wins the argument with his superior intelligence. But also, Disaster: While Will wins the argument, he is still trapped in a lower social strata because inherited wealth is still the top social layer.

- What is the setting for this scene? Why is this an appropriate scene for the action that happens? Harvard Bar. Appropriate because it's a place all levels of society might meet; it's an off-beat or unusual haunt for Will and his friends, so it's also alien territory.
- What are the underlying emotions of this scene? Testing the limits of the social strata; Will's loyalty to his friend; intelligence v. education.
- If you know the larger story, list at least 3 reasons why this is a necessary scene for this story.
  - o Introduces the lead female character.
  - o Thematically, it re-introduces the question of intelligence v. education
  - o Characterizes Will as intelligent, loyal, belligerent.
- What else do you notice about scenes by studying this film clip? The clothing worn by each character also indicates social status. (Add anything else here that you noticed.)

In another example, let's look at *Lizzie Bright and Buckminster's Boy*, by Gary D. Schmidt, a Newbery Honor book. Chapter 3 has these scenes:

- Turner's father, the minister, punishes him for several misdeeds. (2 pages)
- Turner suffers in his room from the summer heat. (Half page)
- Turner survives supper without a misstep. (One page)
- Turner watches the sunset and almost likes Maine. (Half page)

- Turner seeks a place where he "can breathe"; he goes to the seashore. (2 pages)
- Turner meets Lizzie Bright, who teaches him how to bat Maine-style. (6 pages)
- At supper, Turner is lectured by his father until his mother steps in and stops it. (2 pages)
- Turner heads to the hay meadow to play baseball, but a rainstorm stops the game. (1 page)

Several short scenes build up to the longest scene in which Turner, a white boy, meets Lizzie Bright, a black girl, and they become instant friends, something that will cause trouble throughout the rest of the story. Notice that Turner is at the center of each scene and each scene contains conflict, both big and small.

For example, when Turner meets Lizzie Bright, he is throwing stones. She calls to him and in his surprise, his last stone is thrown overhead and comes down and hits his nose. It bleeds, and his bloody shirt will get him in more trouble with the minister in the next scene. In his pain, Turner refuses to answer Lizzie Bright's questions, so she thinks he is an idiot. Besides the overall problem of not liking Maine and befriending the wrong person, Turner has smaller conflicts within the scene itself.

Scenes aren't built just of actions; of course, I am just emphasizing them because it's a common weakness to neglect them. Your scenes will also include dialogue, narrative and interior thoughts. Once you decide on the basic actions, you'll fill out the story with what the characters say, description narrative, narrative that connects or makes transitions, and the interior thoughts of the point-of-view character.

Here are some resources to help you study more about scenes:

1. Pattison, Darcy. "30 Days to a Stronger Scene" series of blog posts on Fiction Notes.

http://www.darcypattison.com/revision/30-days-to-stronger-scenes-series-toc/

2. Scofield, Sandra. *The Scene Book: A Primer for the Fiction Writer*. New York, NY: Penguin 2007.

ESSENTIAL WRITING SKILL #2: VIVID IMAGERY

"Vivid imagery makes a story world come alive," says Stacy Whitman, editorial director of the Tu Books imprint at Lee & Low. Everyone agrees that a writer's ability to create an image in a reader's head through their words is integral to fiction and effective novels. When writers and editors push toward imagery vivid enough to transport readers to new worlds, there are many options.

A book Whitman edited is *In the Serpent's Coils: Hallomere* (Wizards of the Coast, 2007), by Tiffany Trent, the first of a dark-fantasy novel series called *Hallomere*. (Update: Wizards of the Coast is no longer publishing stand-alone fantasy novels and this series is out of print, only available from used book sources.) The series features six girls from around the world who are drawn together to rescue their missing schoolmates and prevent catastrophe in an epic battle between dark fey (or supernatural) worlds and the mortal world.

Whitman describes this short scene as having vivid nature imagery that sets a dreamy, magical mood for the novel, while emphasizing the Fey's connection to nature:

> But then she saw a dark shimmer by the hemlocks again. The tall man turned, as though he felt her gaze. He wore shadows deeper than twilight, and, as before, she couldn't see his face. But she felt his gaze, felt it through the swift gasp of her heart, the seizure in her knees. The Captain raised his hand to her, and she saw, despite the dusk, that his hand was shiny and scarlet, as though wet with blood.

Alan Gratz creates a different sort of mood in his award winning book, *The Samurai Shortstop* (Dial Books, 2006), through what he describes as stark and direct description. In one of the most emotional openings of a story in young adult literature, Toyo helps his Uncle Koji perform the Japanese ritual suicide, *seppuku*.

> *Now Toyo sat in the damp grass outside the shrine as his uncle moved to the center of the mats. Uncle Koji's face was a mask of calm. He wore a ceremonial white kimono with brilliant red wings–the wings he usually wore only into battle. He was clean-shaven and recently bathed, and he wore his hair in a tight topknot like the samurai of old. Uncle Koji knelt on the tatami mats keeping his hands on his hips and his arms akimbo.*

Both Gratz and Trent are paying particular attention to the sensory details used in creating distinct images. Sensory details are those things that a character sees, hears, feels (not emotions, but temperature, texture and kinesthetics), tastes, and smells. As human beings, we understand our world through these senses and including them in a story creates the Show-Don't-Tell imagery that makes a world come alive. Beginning writers often focus on visual details, but it's essential to provide a variety of sensory details. While Gratz's visual details are clear and precise, he also gives us the damp grass and the kinesthetics of how Uncle Koji holds his body.

CHOOSING THE RIGHT DETAILS

What do authors focus on as they try to create vivid imagery? The traditional answer might be to select great adjectives and metaphors. But Gratz offers different advice: Simplify.

Gratz says his first drafts are overwritten and he concentrates on simplifying: "Since *seppuku* is already a startlingly graphic thing, I knew that to overplay it would ruin it. I used the occasional metaphor ('his body deflated like a torn rice sack') but for the most part I presented the ritual steps in almost a clinical fashion. I wanted to show the suicide in the simplest most direct means possible."

He revised numerous times, always with this mantra: simplify, simplify, simplify.

This extended even to the dialogue between the father and son that ends the ritual suicide chapter; Gratz simplified until only five lines, 23-words remained:

> *"Did you watch carefully?" his father asked.*
> *"Hai," Toyo said.*
> *"You observed precisely how it was done?"*
> *"Hai, Father."*
> *"Good," Sotaro Shimada said to his son. "Soon you will do the same for me."*

Strong verbs and specific nouns are the core of the writing; adjectives, adverbs and metaphors are only added as needed.

In other words, authors make choices, selecting the right details. Whitman says, "Improving imagery doesn't just mean becoming more and more observant of the sensory world around you. It also means knowing how to express that imagery. An author can even use too much imagery, muddying the intended effect."

The key is to select, choose, simplify, focus. Whitman says, "Get to the core of the scene." In the *Hallowmere* selection above, the first draft focused on the main character's point of view, what she was seeing. "It pulled the reader away from WHAT Corrine saw, and too much was happening. The core of the scene, the man with the red hand lurking in the shadows, was lost. The revision picked a smaller number of images to narrow in on, allowing those images the strength they need to evoke the mood."

Study this original version to see how the selection above is more focused:

She could see the very edge of the hawthorn if she leaned out far enough. Ghostly light from the hedge flashed in response to the sky above. In one of the flashes, she saw a tall figure standing in front of the hawthorn, and although it was man-shaped, she had the distinct feeling that it wasn't entirely human. She also was quite sure it was looking at her. The being raised its hand towards her. Its outstretched palm glistened in the uncertain light.

IMAGERY THROUGH CHARACTER

Not all authors add imagery automatically; they come to it through a different route. Candie Moonshower, author of *The Legend of Zoey* (Delacorte Press 2006), says she is a character-driven kind of writer. "I have to remind myself to not forget sensory details. My first draft is always a huge info dump–I write fast and furious, spelling out the plot for myself, a bare-bones plot, often, but at least I have the story from which to hang the details. I then go back through and cut all the unnecessary verbiage. On the third draft is when I start asking questions about sensory details and also the psychology of the scene and character."

Moonshower wants to put the reader into the mind and emotions of her character. In this excerpt, Zoey is looking for her mule, King George. Moonshower says, "I focus on showing how the mule's appearance let Zoey know that he'd been through a lot to make it back to her, so I used details such as his ribs showing, his mangy coat and his stinky smell. I also wanted to evoke Zoey's real emotion at seeing her mule-friend again–how very much it means to her that in the midst of her topsy-turvy flight into a chaotic and frightening past, King George the Mule can be counted on."

I took off my shoes and stepped into the creek. The water was frigid, but that didn't stop me. I desperately wanted to catch King George before he ran away again. He still wore his bridle with the reins dangling in front, though his packs had disappeared.

> *In answer, the mule nudged me, hard. I threw my arms around his broad chest and cried into his mangy coat. He was skinny and he stank a bit, but no animal had ever looked as dear to me as King George.*

Details reveal character. Jennifer Wingertzahn, former Editor at Clarion Books, agrees that vivid writing can open up a scene and reveal character. "By showing us a scene–fleshing it out with dialogue, perspective, voice, and language–it opens those characters up and lets the readers see them interact firsthand. Suddenly these characters feel more real because we can hear their voice and see the drama between them for ourselves." She points to Deborah Davis's young adult novel, *Not Like You* (Clarion, 2007) as a book with vivid writing that peels back the layers of characters.

IMAGERY THROUGH STRONG WORD CHOICES

Another route into vivid imagery is by controlling word choices. Katy Duffield, author of *Farmer McPeepers and His Missing Milk Cows* (Rising Moon, 2003) says, "One strong verb can replace several weak words. I concentrate on fun, action words kids will enjoy. It may sound boring, but a neat exercise is to take an old manuscript and change every verb. Often, the tone changes dramatically, making the story more vivid, more accurate, and especially, more fun."

NARRATION AND IMAGERY

Imagery makes scenes come alive; but fiction is created by interweaving narration and scenes that evoke specific imagery. The narration ties together the scenes with information that interprets the events, or, it can function as a transition between scenes. Author Mel Boring says, "The images must not overbear the narrative, so that the images become 'sidetrips' away from the narrative." He points to the *Eragon* series, by Christopher Paolini as an example of vivid images. "Not only are his images sharply vivid, but the narrative transports you to a fantasy setting with scene touches and descriptions that dissolve any barrier to being transported to that fantasy."

Whitman reinforces this idea: "Vivid images are at the service of narration." She offers these examples:

- Clunky narration: *Corrine felt rough hands at the back of her smock tying the laces.*
- Smoother: *Rough hands turned Corrine and tied the laces at the back of her smock.*
- Clunky narration: *Corrine felt that Mara eyed all of them, especially her, with a piercing disregard.*
- Smoother: *Mara eyed all of them, especially Corrine, with a piercing disregard.*

In these examples, it's not necessary to say, "Corrine felt. . ." Instead, give the reader the details straight. Avoid using phrases like "s/he heard," s/he saw," "s/he tasted," or "s/he smelled." Remove that layer of narration.

Moonshower sums it up: "I'm a big fan of purity and simplicity. If I can write imagery in such a way that it speaks to some experience a child has had–whatever that experience might be, and it could be different for each child–and that imagery is intrinsic to the scene and the characters, then I feel I've done my job. When I first started writing for children, I tried to write beautifully and lyrically, but when it is forced, it is often a lot of beautiful lyricism that says nothing to the child reader. Now I try and say it in a way that speaks to the child in me, and I hope that it speaks to other children, too."

You may overwrite or underwrite your first draft, it doesn't matter. If you can manage to bring the story to life with vivid imagery in the first draft, your revisions will be quicker and more efficient. But if you are a writer who bare bones a first draft, just know that you must address this lack of sensory details in the next draft.

CREATING THE RIGHT MOOD

Sensory details are also the doorway to creating a strong mood for a scene. Once again, think about your story and what sensory details. your character would be experiencing. What do they See, Hear, Touch, Taste, Feel?

But this time, you want to select details that support your mood. For example, if you want a scary beach, the sky is dark, brooding; the waves crash so loudly that you can't hear the gulls; the cold wind grounds all seabirds and cuts through your flimsy sweater; the wind blasts your face and you can't get away from the taste of salt; you smell nothing but the wool scarf wrapped around your face.

If you want a happy beach, you choose different details; soft wind ruffles your hair, sunglasses slide down the sweat on your nose, the smell of sunscreen brings back memories of that time on the beach in Jamaica, the *mojita* tastes perfectly minty, and the sea is a glassy swell.

Writers notice sensory details.. Then, they choose the right details to create a mood.

[5]

STEP Three: Plan the Opening Chapter

YOU ARE ALMOST READY TO DIVE IN and write that first chapter. By now, you should have focused your plot and characters and know a lot about where you are going. In Step Three, you'll plan your opening scene and chapter. We'll review some basic concepts about scenes and chapters, dismiss some poor ways to start a story, and then focus on strong ways to start.

CHAPTERS OR SCENES

One question that comes up is whether you should focus on writing your story scene-by-scene or chapter-by-chapter. Scenes are a natural division of a story, while chapters artificially break text into sections. But the relationship between the scene and chapter can be complicated. Sometimes, one scene takes up a chapter, and other times, several scenes combine to create a chapter. Chapters may contain several scenes or just a partial scene. A chapter break may deliberately divide a scene at a crucial place in the story, creating a so-called cliffhanger. Chapters are meant to layout a story in chunks that are easy to consume, giving readers a place to pause.

In his book, *Lessons from a Lifetime of Writing: A Novelist Looks at His Craft*, action/adventure author, David Morrell (creator of the Rambo character, among others), says he tries to write short chapters, so that a reader can complete one chapter (or structural unit) at one sitting. He bases his ideas on two essays by Edgar Allen Poe, "The Philosophy of Composition" and "The Poetic Principle."

Here, Poe is discussing, in part, how to keep a reader's attention.

> *"The initial consideration was that of extent. If any literary work is too long to be read at one sitting, we must be content to dispense with the immensely important effect derivable from unity of impression- for, if two sittings be required, the affairs of the world interfere, and everything like totality is at once destroyed."*

Morrell says he keeps his structural units small in order to accommodate the reader's bladder, TV interruptions, phone calls, a neighbor who drops in, etc. He tries to make sure each chapter has a "unity of impression." He's not concerned with scenes or chapters, but where a story might pause in order to create a unified impression in the reader's mind and where a reader might be enticed to pause and then pick up the reading again. Poe's essays are worth reading, as is Morrell's chapter on "The Tactics of Structure."

In other words, chapters and scenes should be as long as needed, but consider shorter chapters/scenes that can be read at one sitting. Create any reasonable relationship among chapters and scenes that enhances the reader's experience. That is, each scene could be a separate chapter, or a chapter could include several related scenes—those that have the "unity of impression"—that build to some sort of high moment. On the other hand, when you stop a chapter at a cliffhanger, you are actually interrupting a scene, while enhancing the reader's enjoyment of the story.

WEAK WAYS TO START YOUR NOVEL

Now, we will look at some weak ways to start a story, namely by beginning with backstory, flashbacks or starting at the wrong moment.

When we invent characters, we need to know all about them, including where they grew up, childhood fears and dreams and more. Where does this information belong? Where do you put all this backstory?

You might struggle with backstory because of two different reasons. First, you might need to add backstory to enrich the story and the emotional lives of his characters. Second, you might be writing a sequel and the whole previous novel is backstory to the new novel; you can't be sure the reader has read the previous book, though, so you must had to work in some of that story into this one.

BACKSTORY

Many of my thoughts about backstory are shaped by the needs of science fiction and fantasy (sff) writing, where the writer creates a world, complete with complex sociological and political histories and magical norms. The challenge in this genre is to communicate this complex world and culture without stopping for a history lesson. Orson Scott Card has an excellent chapter on handling exposition (and backstory) in his book, *How to Write Science Fiction and Fantasy*.

Basically, new information is filtered through the main viewpoint character. Specific terminology, even if alien and unfamiliar, is helpful; what is named is no longer so confusing. Implication is essential. Often a phenomenon is named, but the explanation isn't given immediately. Sff readers understand this as one of the conventions of the genre and don't mind waiting and pondering the meaning until the right time comes for an explanation. My friend who writes middle-grade non-fiction chaffs under the sff conventions because she feels that the explanation must come immediately and be placed right next to the unfamiliar term. But for fiction, terms can be understood partially in context and the sff reader waits, knowing more is coming.

So, I come from a reading background of understanding huge chunks of backstory through the techniques of implication, slow revealing of complexities or intrigue, and I'm comfortable with a certain degree of ambiguity, as long as I trust the author that the answers will come eventually. It's part of the appeal of the genre (and why many dislike it!). So, before we even start the discussion of where to put backstory, I'm comfortable with delaying it a long while, both as a reader and as a writer. But I want to emphasize that the reader must never be confused about what is happening in the story. The reader may not understand exactly what a *bligfa* is, but should understand its function in this scene. Clarity must rule, even if everything is not understood.

One of the clichés of contemporary stories is a first chapter with lots of immediate action and a second chapter of backstory. Literary agent Donald Maass rails against this practice in *Writing the Breakout Novel Workbook*:

> *"Again and again in manuscripts I find my eyes skimming over backstory passages in chapters one, two and even three. Backstory doesn't engage me because it doesn't tell a story. It does not have tension to it, usually, or complicate problems."*

"Ideally, all fiction should seem to be happening now," echoes Sol Stein in *Stein on Writing*.

DISADVANTAGES OF EARLY BACKSTORY
- Pulls the reader out of the current time flow.
- Bogs down the opening, destroying the pacing.

- Backstory tends to "tell" a story instead of "show" it, a weak narrative strategy.
- The use of flashbacks for backstory is often awkwardly handled. We will discuss this more in a minute.

ADVANTAGES OF BACKSTORY

- Deepen inner conflict. Backstory can provide motivation for the conflict, deepen the emotional effects and let the reader empathize with even the villain.
- Increase tension. Hinting at backstory, but not telling all makes readers long to know the "secrets," too. We read on to find out what secret is so terrible that it provides the motivation for this conflict.

Usually backstory, especially a flashback, should be put at a point where it will enhance the tension and conflict of the story. You can think of a story of as a collection of scenes, followed by characters reacting emotionally to events, then reflecting upon the scene and deciding what to do next, which leads to the next scene. Scene, emotions, reflection, decision, scene. Often the backstory needs to come during that in-between stage where the character is reacting emotionally to the events of the scene that has just happened.

For example, Gloria slaps Joe. So what? What are the readers supposed to make of that? What does it mean? We don't know; the author must help the reader interpret the action in some way. The scene could progress without the explanation until Joe turns around and makes a fast exit. Then, Gloria has the time to react emotionally. That's the point for a flashback that explains that Joe once accused her of embezzling money and let her stand trial, even though it was Joe who had stolen the money.

Ah, now the backstory explains and deepens the tension. But an early chapter that goes into a long story of how Gloria and Joe worked together for many years and Joe was Gloria's mentor and they even had a brief affair that Gloria's husband still doesn't know about—that's bogs down the pacing. It doesn't help Gloria make a decision about what to do next. It doesn't add to the present conflict, even if it does explain it somewhat.

WHERE DO YOU PUT BACKSTORY?

Backstory is there for its emotional weight. The story's current situation is emotional, but for some reason you want to up the stakes. By adding backstory, you can strengthen the motivations of the character and make events mean more. Backstory should add irony, poignancy, regret, hope, or other strong emotions.

That means you put backstory at the point where it most directly impacts the emotions of the characters and/or the reader.

BUT WHERE EXACTLY DO YOU PUT BACKSTORY?

You put the backstory at the point where it impacts the emotional weight of the story. Exactly there. For example, can you interrupt a scene with backstory? Yes. But you'd better have a strong emotional reason to slow down the story at that point.

How does backstory impact the story's emotional weight?

1. Interpret actions/dialogue/events. Some scenes, such as an action scene, are better left intact with any flashbacks or backstory coming later as the character reflects on the events. Then, the flashback helps the character interpret the scene's importance or outcome.

2. Help make a decision. Sometimes, though, a scene leads up to a character making a decision. Flashbacks provide needed information and emotion to help the character make the best (or worst) decision.

3. Change relationships. If the backstory comes in dialogue, instead of as a flashback, it can change relationships.

4. Story twist. If your plot is too straight-line, a good bit of backstory can add an interesting twist on events. What? Darth Vader is Luke Skywalker's father?

FLASHBACKS EFFECTIVE IN DEEPENING A NOVEL

Flashbacks, scenes or partial scenes of something that happened before this moment in the story timeline, are the best way to insert backstory. In other words, a flashback is a scene that is presented out of chronological order. The flashback relates to the current scene, deepens character motivations, or otherwise illuminates the current action of the novel.

First, write the scene with the current action and make it as fully developed as possible. If you're going to interrupt the on-going action of the novel to insert this backstory then at least give the reader a full scene that will keep their interest.

Then, write the flashback as a fully developed scene. Since you are messing with the time line or chronology of the novel, it should be done in such a way to keep the reader's interest. This doesn't mean it has to take up pages; a paragraph of a mini-scene might be perfectly reasonable. On the other hand, the flashback might need to be several pages long in your novel. Do what works.

Now, integrate the two scenes. Figure out where exactly in the novel the reader needs this bit of backstory in order to understand the story's action or to create a deeper emotional response. Put the flashback as close to that as you can. Then smooth out the transitions.

For example, Cinderella's mother died in childbirth, and the baby, the sister that Cinderella might have had, also died. The flashback to the birth scene, where Cinderella tells her mother—and sister—goodbye should be placed at the point at which Cinderella learns that Prince Phillipe has just proposed to her step-sister Belinda. The loss of the baby sister is contrasted with the reality of the sister in front of her: will Cinderella embrace this girl as her "real" sister or not? This doesn't belong in chapter one! It belongs right in the midst of the emotional reaction to Belinda's joyful moment.

The trickiest part of a flashback is getting into in and out of it. Try to do it with a single sentence both times. One transitional opening sentence should signal a time shift, and then go straight into past tense like you would in any scene of a novel.

> *I remember that cloudy evening, the night before the tornado. Dogs whined restlessly, cattle kicked over buckets of full milk, and chickens scratched endlessly at the dust, all warnings that something bad was coming.*

Coming out of it, use a single transition sentence again.

> *I walked away without a scratch on the outside, but felt like a stray splinter of wood had stabbed my heart. Now, looking at Jeremiah, the coward of that night of horror, I couldn't believe he was asking me to be brave.*

This demonstrates that a flashback scene needs to be a high point or a low point in a character's life, something worthy of a dedicated flashback. There also needs to be some emotional hook. Here, you can sense that the Jeremiah's behavior during the tornado was cowardly, and that affects the current scene.

WAYS THAT FLASHBACKS GO WRONG

1. Too early. Too often, I see a flashback in the second paragraph of the opening scene. No! If you need that flashback in the second paragraph, you have started in the wrong place. Or, I may see one on the second page. No! Or the entire second chapter is a flashback. No! Only use a flashback at the point where it will directly impact the ongoing action.

2. Too much exposition. Flashbacks should give the reader a scene, not pages of compressed exposition. Work the facts the reader needs to know into the flashback portion of the scene just like you would into any scene.

3. Watch verb tenses. The conditional tense that uses the "would" construction is awkward and should be avoided in flashbacks. Sometimes, you want to indicate that, for example, watching fireflies in the evening was a habit of your family. You write something like this:

> *Every evening we <u>would</u> gather on the lawn and wait for dusk. We <u>would</u> slap at a few mosquitoes, <u>would</u> murmur quietly in the heat, and <u>would</u> sip ice tea. We <u>would</u> wait until the fireflies <u>would</u> start winking, and then the chase <u>would</u> begin.*

That's too awkward, with seven repetitions of "would." Instead, use the one "would" construction and go straight into the past tense. Use a single "would" to come out of it.

> *Every evening we <u>would</u> gather on the lawn and wait for dusk. We slapped at a few mosquitoes, murmured quietly in the heat and sipped ice tea. We waited until the fireflies started winking and the chase <u>would</u> begin.*

4. No connetcions. The flashback has no connection to the current time in the novel. Why include this flashback? It must up the stakes, provide motivation, increase the emotional tension; it must relate to the current novel in a vital way. If it doesn't do this, if it's just there to give us a history lesson, cut it.

OTHER DEAD END WAYS TO START A CHAPTER

WAKING UP. Rarely does it work to have a character start a novel in bed, and then wake up. Boring.

DON'T GIVE AWAY THE ENDING. Another weak way to begin is to give away the ending of the story. The best advice I've heard is that stories should begin at a point of innocence.

Don't start with something like this: "It was the worst day of my life." That robs the reader of entering a situation as an innocent, not knowing what to expect. It lessens tension, suspense and conflict. Not a good thing to do. It's jumping the timeline, foreshadowing to your own detriment. Yes, sometimes a skilled writer can pull it off because it signals to the reader what sort of story this is going to be, a tragedy. But usually, it winds up spoiling the surprises planned for the reader.

Instead, readers want to experience a situation from the main character or narrator's point of view with a blow-by-blow, as-it-happens narration of events. Yes, it's fine to include some of the main character's or narrator's attitude; in fact, it's essential. The experience must be colored with rose-colored or jealous-green glasses, or whatever is appropriate for your story. That's expected and it enhances the reader's experience of the story.

Orson Scott Card says it a different way when he suggests that the only thing you withhold from a reader is what happens next. We know where we are, who is there, when we are, and why we are here. The only thing we don't know is what happens next. THAT is where tension comes from.

SUMMARY OF SCENE. Similar to giving away the ending is the tendency to provide a summary. Consider:

> *Emily knocked on Bruce's door. She just had to make it through his Christmas party.*

Here, we're told in a summary statement what the upcoming scene will entail: "making it through his Christmas party." Instead, let the reader experience the party for themselves.

> *Emily knocked on Bruce's door and entered. She wanted to plug her ears against the jazzed up Christmas carols that blasted above the crowd noise. She edged around the room's perimeter toward the punch table, avoiding an elbow here and barely keeping a cowboy boot from stomping on her foot there, hoping to find someone familiar.*

In this opening, the reader experiences the party with Emily. Leaving out the summary statement about making it through the party strengthens the reader's curiosity about what happens next. That's the only thing we leave in question: what happens next? Don't undercut this natural curiosity by summarizing the action before you present it. Time enough later for Emily to gripe to Joe about the lousy party.

TRYING TOO HARD TO GRAB THE READER. These type openings start with something startling. There's nothing wrong with that except that often the event comes from nowhere and goes nowhere. It's only there for shock value and the reader is left wondering where we are and why we are there. And why should the reader care? Car wrecks—from which the main characters walk away unscathed—are rather ho-hum.

NOT ENOUGH CONTEXT. Part of the problem in this type opening is the reader isn't oriented. Where are we? Think of time of day, time of year, geographic location, stage of a relationship. The setting should be clearly evoked in the opening, the situation should be recognizable, the emotional landscape should be crystal clear.

ACTION/REACTION SEQUENCE OUT OF ORDER. Finally, the events might be out of order. The normal sequence of events is action-thought/emotion-reaction. In an attempt to catch a reader's attention, though, writers are tempted to give the reaction first.

> *Terry screamed.*

The reader has no idea why someone screamed and in order to explain, you must backtrack, essentially a mini-flashback. Not good.

> *Walking down the wooded path, Terry tripped. She screamed.*

Now, the reader has the action-reaction in a clear sequence, not confused but just as hooked. Notice that we also have a hint at setting.

If you want, you can add an emotion.

> *Walking down the wooded path, Terry tripped. Falling, she thought of her new ballet slippers waiting for tonight's rehearsal and if she hurt herself in the fall she would never have another chance to dance for the King. She screamed.*

Now, events are in the correct time sequence, we know where we are, and why we should care.

DULL VOCABULARY. If there's ever a place for brilliance of voice, phrasing, interesting vocabulary, it's the opening of a novel. Here is where you want to catch a reader's attention. No, you don't want it to be so overblown that it is out of character with the rest of the story; however, you do want it to catch the reader. And, the beauty is that if you do overwrite, it's just a first draft.

CONFLICT, THE MOMENT BEFORE AND PROPHETIC OPENINGS

We've covered some weak ways to open a novel. Now, let's look at strong strategies for an opening. Characters aren't just plopped down onto a first page. Instead, your characters have been living their lives, working, eating, sleeping. Before you write that first sentence, consider what the character was doing just a moment ago, right before you picked up their story line.

Openings, like every scene, should also be fraught with a feeling for "the moment before." That is, the subtext of the story, even in the opening, should be imbued with the characters hopes, dreams, experiences, joys, triumphs, dangers, and more. What happened just before this opening scene? How does that affect the emotional content of this scene?

Characters need to make an entrance into scenes, especially the opening scene, with an attitude and that comes from what happened just before this point in the story. They don't come out of nowhere. That doesn't mean you write all that pre-story or backstory, unless it is just for yourself; but pre-story does color the scene with attitude.

Ruta Sepetys' novel, *Between Shades of Gray*, is a World War II story that opens in Lithuania, in June, 1941 with Lina's family arrested by the NKVD, the Soviet secret police. Her family has been making preparations to escape when the police barge in. Just the moment before, though, Lina had changed into her nightgown and sat down to write a letter to her cousin. It's a normal night for her, which make the knocking, the "urgent booming," on the door even more startling and poignant.

Stories must have conflict and that must begin on page one. The first chapter must start the conflict of the story, enough conflict to hook a reader. It's tricky to find the right opening scene. You may need to write some early exploratory pages that are trial runs for how to handle characters, voice, settings, and events. Often these lack any tension; they are just vignettes. During the Messy Phase of planning a novel, write as many of these exploratory drafts as needed, but recognize their purpose as helping you to hone your ideas for the story. They are not your opening chapter.

On the other hand, in an attempt to jump-start a story, early drafts often open with a dramatic action scene. The problem here is that the reader doesn't have any emotional connection to the characters yet, and, well, so what? Why should a reader care if character A dies horribly? It is conflict, but not with characters that the reader cares about. Finding the right starting point is a matter of balancing conflict with character.

Another problem with the early drafts is an intense focus on the current scene.

> "They murdered him."
>
> Opening line from The Chocolate Wars by Robert Cormier.

In the opening scene of *The Chocolate Wars*, the main character is playing football, in spite of being too skinny, too small. He gets smashed into the ground; hence, "They murdered him." At the end of the novel, the "Chocolate Gang" literally beats up the main character, in a different interpretation of the phrase. The Prophetic Opening contains the ending in encapsulated form, it looks past the current scene, but doesn't give too much away.

You can focus on imagery as a way to find the right Prophetic Openings for your story. For example, at a retreat I taught, one writer took her characters to Florida so the brother could participate in dolphin therapy for his muscular dystrophy. However, the opening lines talked about how dolphins assist in the care of their young. "Dolphin aunts" often nudge a newborn to the surface for his/her first breath.

Wow, it was a great opening, with vivid imagery. But—what does that have to do with muscular dystrophy? If the muscles were the focus, then something about the dolphin's muscles would be more appropriate.

Ah—but what if, the brother had cystic fibrosis, a disorder that affects breathing, instead of muscular dystrophy? Then, the image of helping a newborn dolphin breathe takes on new meaning in the story. In this case, the writer wasn't wedded to the idea of muscular dystrophy and chose to go with the new breathing disorder. If muscular dystrophy had been her focus, though, she could have changed the opening imagery.

Another writer had a story that incorporated farming. We talked about various imagery she might use: firing a field to get it ready for planting and then continuing fire as a cleansing image or as a "home fires" image; taproots of native grasses that sink twenty feet into the ground, making the prairie able to withstand all sorts of disasters; farming tools and implements, such as plows or tractors. Maybe you've got a story about how a family is the stable force in a teen's life. Then begin with a description of the prairie grasses taproots and liken that to the family genealogy in some way.

In other words, look at what you've already got in your story and see if there is imagery available to use. Keep it integral to the story elements but bring it forward some to create imagery and symbols that hold power within your story. Craft a prophetic opening that sets up the ending.

Let The Reader Participate

Sara Pennypacker is the author of the *Clementine* series of early-chapter books. Her books are widely recognized as a forte in capturing the reader and drawing them in. The opening scene of Book 1 has Clementine, a third grade dynamo, sitting in the principal's office and a frequent comment is that the scene is hilarious.

But Pennypacker says she didn't write it humorous. Rather, the reader wrote it funny. What does she mean?

Consider this line:

> *Someone should tell you not to answer the phone in the principal's office, if that's a rule.*

It's funny. You know from this line that Clementine has answered the principal's phone line and it resulted in disaster. Even without details or without the usual "Show-Don't-Tell," it's funny. But the humor is created in the reader's mind, by the reader's imagination.

The technique of leaving out the most dramatic part in favor of letting the reader create meaning is useful, especially in opening lines. The danger is when it's used too often or if it is used as a lazy crutch or excuse for not Show-Don't-Telling. In other words, most of the time the important details should be shown, not told. But sometimes, leaving out details and letting the reader fill them in is OK. It's effective in *Clementine*'s opening page because it fits Clementine's voice as a naive character and because Pennypacker already gave the reader specific details: the school served Hamburger Surprise at lunch, and Margaret's mother was coming to get her because Clementine did something bad to Margaret's hair.

Also, while what is left out is not specific, it is absolutely clear. The reader is not confused by having something left out. Clarity rules.

Notice, though, that this introduction is swiftly followed by a conventional scene with a stricter adherence to the Show-Don't-Tell maxim. Used too often, leaving out the most dramatic part would just confuse the reader.

Pennypacker had a hard task, not only to introduce a specific scene, but to set up a voice, a character, a situation, and eventually a series of books about this endearing third grader. She succeeded by letting the reader participate in creating humor.

Use a Mentor Text

One strategy for starting a novel is to find examples to emulate, to find what educators call a "mentor text." Thinking in general terms, consider your story's basic topic, theme, setting and genre and look around at different stories that might echo yours in some way. For this, you don't care if the mentor text is a horror story, a Young Adult romance, or some other genre. Instead, search for strategies to open a story with conflict. Your main criteria should be "conflict on every page," but you can add other criteria, depending on your story. You may want a mentor text with a description in the opening paragraph. Or, you may want a mentor text that opens with dialogue.

After you locate several mentor texts, imitate the texts in some trial drafts. In one story, I used a classic text and actually ripped off the first sentence (which I may or may not eventually keep). That is, I followed the sentence structure exactly: adjective, noun, verb, prepositional phrase. I didn't use the exact words the mentor text did, but I tried to find similar-sounding words to get a true echo. The result was a different sort of opening that leaves much unsaid but also hints at much.

Will I keep it? It's a good enough first line and opening paragraph to move on to the rest of the story. I won't know if I'll keep it, though, until the final revisions are done. For now, it's a solid start that feels right enough that I can work on chapter two. That's your goal for your first draft of a first chapter: a solid enough piece of writing to pull you to the next chapter.

Let's prepare for the opening line of your story.

Totally Stuck? 3 Assignments to Get Unstuck

For those who are still struggling to know where to start, write something using these three strategies and then choose your favorite. The main goal right now is to get something on the page, to get your story going. Here are your three assignments:

1. SENSORY DETAILS. Decide where your character is in the opening chapter, then close your eyes, put yourself there and try to imagine all the things the character might see, hear, touch, taste or smell. Then, push hard to find an interesting detail and start writing there. The danger is that you might start with too much description. That's

OK, you can take care of that during revision. The goal here is to get started.

2. ACTION. Alternatively, starting with a great verb can help jumpstart the story. Think beyond the usual: walk, run, turn head, whirl. Instead, go for something distinctive: salute, pirouette, regurgitate. (Please, avoid those pesky adverbs, which add so little. Not walked lazily. But strolled.) Get your character in motion, and keep him/her in motion for a page or so, and you'll figure out where to go next.

3. DIALOGUE. One of my favorite openings to a novel is *Tom Sawyer*, which opens with his aunt calling: "Tom!" Begin with a bit of dialogue. Keep it going for about ten exchanges and then move on.

[6]

STEP FOUR: Plan the Opening Line

You are now ready to write the first sentence of your novel. It's an important sentence, because it should pull the reader on to the next sentence. In an article for the *Writer's Chronicle,* Susan Lumenello explains twelve strategies for opening lines. [1]

1. It was. . . It is. . . This is. . .
2. Viewpoint on Life
3. Mid-action
4. Spoken word or dialogue
5. Landscape
6. Set-up
7. Let's meet Jack or Jill
8. Let's meet Joe, my friend.
9. I AM
10. Misleading lines
11. Alternative Media
12. Screenplay or Graphic Novel format

I've expanded her twelve strategies in detail below by illustrating them with the "100 Best Lines from Novels," as chosen by the editors of the *American Book Review*.[2]

I made decisions about how to categorize each quote, but it wasn't easy. For example, "Elmer Gantry was drunk." This could be an introduction to the character, or it could be starting in mid-action. I categorized it as mid-action, but if you argue for the other, I'd agree. Feel free to disagree: the point is that these include many successful strategies for starting a story, not whether I categorized them right!

You will want to skim through the strategies for ideas for your opening lines. Try to find a couple that appeal to you and then study those examples in detail. After you do that, read through the case study of trying out twelve opening lines.

1. IT WAS...IT IS...THIS IS...

These openings give a writer freedom and flexibility because anything can come after these words: abstract images, a synopsis, a setting, etc. To the reader, this opening signals authority. The possible downside is over familiarity with the opening, so that it reads as a cliché.

- It is a truth universally acknowledged, that a single man in possession of a good fortune, must be in want of a wife. (Jane Austen, *Pride and Prejudice*, c. 1813.)
- It was a bright cold day in April, and the clocks were striking thirteen. (*George Orwell*, 1984, c. 1949.)
- It was the best of times, it was the worst of times, it was the age of wisdom, it was the age of foolishness, it was the epoch of belief, it was the epoch of incredulity, it was the season of Light, it was the season of Darkness, it was the spring of hope, it was the winter of despair. (Charles Dickens, *A Tale of Two Cities*, c. 1859.)

- This is the saddest story I have ever heard. (Ford Madox Ford, *The Good Soldier*, c. 1915.)

- It was a dark and stormy night; the rain fell in torrents, except at occasional intervals, when it was checked by a violent gust of wind which swept up the streets (for it is in London that our scene. lies), rattling along the house-tops, and fiercely agitating the scanty flame of the lamps that struggled against the darkness. (Edward George Bulwer-Lytton. *Paul Clifford*, c. 1830.)

- It was a wrong number that started it, the telephone ringing three times in the dead of night, and the voice on the other end asking for someone he was not. (Paul Auster. *City of Glass*, c. 1985.)

- 124 was spiteful. (Toni Morrison, *Beloved*, c. 1987.)

- It was like so, but wasn't. (Richard Powers, *Galatea 2.2*, c. 1995.)

- It was the day my grandmother exploded. (Iain M. Banks, *The Crow Road*, c. 1992.)

- It was a pleasure to burn. (Ray Bradbury, *Fahrenheit 451*, c. 1953.)

- It was love at first sight. (Joseph Heller, *Catch-22*, c. 1961.)

- It was a queer, sultry summer, the summer they electrocuted the Rosenbergs, and I didn't know what I was doing in New York. (Sylvia Plath, *The Bell Jar*, c. 1963.)

- It was just noon that Sunday morning when the sheriff reached the jail with Lucas Beauchamp though the whole town (the whole county too for that matter) had known since the night before that Lucas had killed a white man. (William Faulkner, *Intruder in the Dust*, c. 1948.)

2. VIEWPOINT ON LIFE

Some stories open by presenting "my philosophy of life." This gives a story instant structure, because the author must prove/disprove the thesis presented. It's a bit old-fashioned in tone, but there are still some quotes included from the 1980s and 1990s.

- Happy families are all alike; every unhappy family is unhappy in its own way. (Leo Tolstoy (trans. Constance Garnett), *Anna Karenina*, c.1877.)
- Whether I shall turn out to be the hero of my own life, or whether that station will be held by anybody else, these pages must show. (Charles Dickens, *David Copperfield*, c.1850.)
- The moment one learns English, complications set in. (Felipe Alfau, *Chromos*, c. 1990.)
- Dr. Weiss, at forty, knew that her life had been ruined by literature. (Anita Brookner, *The Debut*, c.1981.)
- Ships at a distance have every man's wish on board. (Zora Neale Hurston, *Their Eyes Were Watching God*, c.1937.)
- We started dying before the snow, and like the snow, we continued to fall. (Louise Erdrich, *Tracks*, c.1988.)
- A story has no beginning or end; arbitrarily one chooses that moment of experience from which to look back or from which to look ahead. (Graham Greene, *The End of the Affair*, c.1951.)
- The human race, to which so many of my readers belong, has been playing at children's games from the beginning, and will probably do it till the end, which is a nuisance for the few people who grow up. (G. K. Chesterton, *The Napoleon of Notting Hill*, c.1904.)
- Most really pretty girls have pretty ugly feet, and so does Mindy Metalman, Lenore notices, all of a sudden. (David Foster Wallace, *The Broom of the System*, c.1987.)

- The past is a foreign country; they do things differently there. (L. P. Hartley, *The Go-Between*, c.1953.)
- Justice?—You get justice in the next world, in this world you have the law. (William Gaddis, *A Frolic of His Own*, c.1994.)
- Of all the things that drive men to sea, the most common disaster, I've come to learn, is women. (Charles Johnson, *Middle Passage*, c.1990.)
- Time is not a line but a dimension, like the dimensions of space. (Margaret Atwood, *Cat's Eye*, c.1988.)
- They say when trouble comes close ranks, and so the white people did. (Jean Rhys, *Wide Sargasso Sea*, c.1966.)

3. MID-ACTION

This opening starts right in the middle of some action, the middle of a scene. It assumes that the reader will care about the characters. It risks having the reader asking, "Who cares?" instead of, "Why?"

- A screaming comes across the sky. (Thomas Pynchon, *Gravity's Rainbow*, c.1973.)
- The Miss Lonelyhearts of the New York Post-Dispatch (Are you in trouble?--Do-you-need-advice?--Write-to-Miss-Lonelyhearts-and-she-will-help-you) sat at his desk and stared at a piece of white cardboard. (Nathanael West, *Miss Lonelyhearts*, c.1933.)
- Stately, plump Buck Mulligan came from the stairhead, bearing a bowl of lather on which a mirror and a razor lay crossed. (James Joyce, *Ulysses*, c.1922.)
- One summer afternoon Mrs. Oedipa Maas came home from a Tupperware party whose hostess had put perhaps too much kirsch in the fondue to find that she, Oedipa, had been named executor, or she supposed executrix, of the estate of one Pierce Inverarity, a California real estate

mogul who had once lost two million dollars in his spare time but still had assets numerous and tangled enough to make the job of sorting it all out more than honorary. (Thomas Pynchon, *The Crying of Lot 49*, c.1966.)

- Through the fence, between the curling flower spaces, I could see them hitting. (William Faulkner, *The Sound and the Fury*, c.1929.)

- Once an angry man dragged his father along the ground through his own orchard. "Stop!" cried the groaning old man at last, "Stop! I did not drag my father beyond this tree." (Gertrude Stein, *The Making of Americans*, c.1925.)

- Mrs. Dalloway said she would buy the flowers herself. (Virginia Woolf, *Mrs. Dalloway*, c.1925.)

- Ages ago, Alex, Allen and Alva arrived at Antibes, and Alva allowing all, allowing anyone, against Alex's admonition, against Allen's angry assertion: another African amusement . . . anyhow, as all argued, an awesome African army assembled and arduously advanced against an African anthill, assiduously annihilating ant after ant, and afterward, Alex astonishingly accuses Albert as also accepting Africa's antipodal ant annexation. (Walter Abish, *Alphabetical Africa*, c.1974.)

- Elmer Gantry was drunk. (Sinclair Lewis, *Elmer Gantry*, c.1927.)

- You better not never tell nobody but God. (Alice Walker, *The Color Purple*, c.1982.)

- Francis Marion Tarwater's uncle had been dead for only half a day when the boy got too drunk to finish digging his grave and a Negro named Buford Munson, who had come to get a jug filled, had to finish it and drag the body from the breakfast table where it was still sitting and bury it in a decent and Christian way, with the sign of its Saviour at the head of the grave and enough dirt on top to keep the dogs from digging it up. (Flannery O'Connor, *The Violent Bear it Away*, c.1960.)

- I write this sitting in the kitchen sink. (Dodie Smith, *I Capture the Castle*, c.1948.)
- He--for there could be no doubt of his sex, though the fashion of the time did something to disguise it--was in the act of slicing at the head of a Moor which swung from the rafters. (Virginia Woolf, *Orlando*, c.1928.)

4. SPOKEN WORD–DIALOGUE

By starting with dialogue, the story signals that this is a novel of relationships and of truth-telling or of its opposite. It can be risky because the reader must immediately care about these characters.

- Money . . . in a voice that rustled. (William Gaddis, *J R*, c.1975.)
- "To be born again," sang Gibreel Farishta tumbling from the heavens, "first you have to die." (Salman Rushdie, *The Satanic Verses*, c.1988.)
- "Take my camel, dear," said my Aunt Dot, as she climbed down from this animal on her return from High Mass. (Rose Macaulay, *The Towers of Trebizon*, c.1956.)
- "When your mama was the geek, my dreamlets," Papa would say, "she made the nipping off of noggins such a crystal mystery that the hens themselves yearned toward her, waltzing around her, hypnotized with longing." (Katherine Dunn, *Geek Love*, c.1983.)

5. LANDSCAPE

Some stories open with the setting, especially some description of landscape. This opening signals the importance of place and how similar or different a character is within a particular place.

- The sun shone, having no alternative, on the nothing new. (Samuel Beckett, *Murphy*, c.1938.)
- Once upon a time and a very good time it was there was a moocow coming down along the road and this moocow that was coming down along the road met a nicens little boy named baby tuckoo. (James Joyce, *A Portrait of the Artist as a Young Man*, c.1916.)
- The sky above the port was the color of television, tuned to a dead channel. (William Gibson, *Neuromancer*, c.1984.)
- In the late summer of that year we lived in a house in a village that looked across the river and the plain to the mountains. (Ernest Hemingway, *A Farewell to Arms*, c.1929.)
- The towers of Zenith aspired above the morning mist; austere towers of steel and cement and limestone, sturdy as cliffs and delicate as silver rods. (Sinclair Lewis, *Babbitt*, c.1922.)
- The cold passed reluctantly from the earth, and the retiring fogs revealed an army stretched out on the hills, resting. (Stephen Crane, *The Red Badge of Courage*, c.1895.)

6. SET UP

This is almost a catchall category, in which the story is set up someway. Sometimes, I put a quote here because it embodies several of the other types of openings, and in the end, it is easier to put it here than repeat it in several places. This is the most blatant story-telling style. It also allows a fast start to a story.

- Many years later, as he faced the firing squad, Colonel Aureliano Buendía was to remember that distant afternoon when his father took him to discover ice. (Gabriel García

Márquez (trans. Gregory Rabassa), *One Hundred Years of Solitude*, c.1967.)

- riverrun, past Eve and Adam's, from swerve of shore to bend of bay, brings us by a commodius vicus of recirculation back to Howth Castle and Environs. (James Joyce, *Finnegans Wake*, c.1939.)

- You don't know about me without you have read a book by the name of The Adventures of Tom Sawyer; but that ain't no matter. (Mark Twain, *Adventures of Huckleberry Finn*, c.1885.)

- Someone must have slandered Josef K., for one morning, without having done anything truly wrong, he was arrested. (Franz Kafka (trans. Breon Mitchell), *The Trial*, c.1925.)

- You are about to begin reading Italo Calvino's new novel. If on a winter's night a traveler. (Italo Calvino (trans. William Weaver), *If on a winter's night a traveler*, c.1979.)

- If you really want to hear about it, the first thing you'll probably want to know is where I was born, and what my lousy childhood was like, and how my parents were occupied and all before they had me, and all that David Copperfield kind of crap, but I don't feel like going into it, if you want to know the truth. (J. D. Salinger, *The Catcher in the Rye*, c.1951.)

- I wish either my father or my mother, or indeed both of them, as they were in duty both equally bound to it, had minded what they were about when they begot me; had they duly considered how much depended upon what they were then doing;—that not only the production of a rational Being was concerned in it, but that possibly the happy formation and temperature of his body, perhaps his genius and the very cast of his mind;—and, for aught they knew to the contrary, even the fortunes of his whole house might take their turn from the humours and dispositions which were then uppermost:--Had they duly weighed and considered all this, and proceeded accordingly,--I am verily persuaded I should have made a quite different figure in the world, from that, in which the reader is likely to see me. (Laurence Sterne, *Tristram Shandy*, c.1759–1767.)

- Every summer Lin Kong returned to Goose Village to divorce his wife, Shuyu. (Ha Jin, *Waiting*, c.1999.)
- Where now? Who now? When now? (Samuel Beckett (trans. Patrick Bowles), *The Unnamable*, c.1953.)
- All this happened, more or less. (Kurt Vonnegut, *Slaughterhouse-Five*, c.1969.)
- They shoot the white girl first. (Toni Morrison, *Paradise*, c.1998.)
- For a long time, I went to bed early. (Marcel Proust (trans. Lydia Davis), *Swann's Way*, c.1913.)
- I was the shadow of the waxwing slain / By the false azure in the windowpane; (Vladimir Nabokov, *Pale Fire*, c.1962.)
- I had the story, bit by bit, from various people, and, as generally happens in such cases, each time it was a different story. (Edith Wharton, *Ethan Frome*, c.1911.)
- Having placed in my mouth sufficient bread for three minutes' chewing, I withdrew my powers of sensual perception and retired into the privacy of my mind, my eyes and face assuming a vacant and preoccupied expression. (Flann O'Brien, *At Swim-Two-Birds*, c.1939.)
- I was born in the Year 1632, in the City of York, of a good Family, tho' not of that Country, my Father being a Foreigner of Bremen, who settled first at Hull; He got a good Estate by Merchandise, and leaving off his Trade, lived afterward at York, from whence he had married my Mother,

whose Relations were named Robinson, a very good Family in that Country, and from whom I was called Robinson Kreutznaer; but by the usual Corruption of Words in England, we are now called, nay we call our selves, and write our Name Crusoe, and so my Companions always call'd me. (Daniel Defoe, *Robinson Crusoe*, c.1719.)

- In the beginning, sometimes I left messages in the street. (David Markson, *Wittgenstein's Mistress*, c.1988.)

- I have never begun a novel with more misgiving. (W. Somerset Maugham, *The Razor's Edge*, c.1944.)

- In my younger and more vulnerable years my father gave me some advice that I've been turning over in my mind ever since. (F. Scott Fitzgerald, *The Great Gatsby*, c.1925.)

- Hiram Clegg, together with his wife Emma and four friends of the faith from Randolph Junction, were summoned by the Spirit and Mrs. Clara Collins, widow of the beloved Nazarene preacher Ely Collins, to West Condon on the weekend of the eighteenth and nineteenth of April, there to await the End of the World. (Robert Coover, *The Origin of the Brunists*, c.1966.)

- On my naming day when I come 12 I gone front spear and kilt a wyld boar he parbly ben the las wyld pig on the Bundel Downs any how there hadnt ben none for a long time befor him nor I aint looking to see none agen. (Russell Hoban, *Riddley Walker*, c.1980.)

- Vaughan died yesterday in his last car-crash. (J. G. Ballard, *Crash*, c.1973.)

- Psychics can see the color of time it's blue. (Ronald Sukenick, *Blown Away*, c.1986.)

- In the town, there were two mutes and they were always together. (Carson McCullers, *The Heart is a Lonely Hunter*, c.1940.)

- Once upon a time two or three weeks ago, a rather stubborn and determined middle-aged man decided to record for posterity, exactly as it happened, word by word and step by step, the story of another man for indeed what is great in man is that he is a bridge and not a goal, a somewhat paranoiac fellow unmarried, unattached, and quite irresponsible, who had decided to lock himself in a room a furnished room with a private bath, cooking facilities, a bed, a table, and at least one chair, in New York City, for a year 365 days to be precise, to write the story of another person--a shy young man about of 19 years old--who, after the war the Second World War, had come to America the land of opportunities from France under the sponsorship of his uncle--a journalist, fluent in five languages--who himself had come to America from Europe Poland it seems, though this was not clearly established sometime during the war after a series of rather gruesome adventures, and who, at the end of the war, wrote to the father his cousin by marriage of the young man whom he considered as a nephew, curious to know if he the father and his family had survived the German occupation, and indeed was deeply saddened to learn, in a letter from the young man--a long and touching letter written in English, not by the young man, however, who did not know a damn word of English, but by a good friend of his who had studied English in school--that his parents both his father and mother and his two sisters one older and the other younger than he had been deported they were Jewish to a German concentration camp Auschwitz probably and never returned, no doubt having been exterminated deliberately X * X * X * X, and that, therefore, the young man who was now an orphan, a displaced person, who, during the war, had managed to escape deportation by working very hard on a farm in Southern France, would be happy and grateful to be given the opportunity to come to America that great country he had heard so much about and yet knew so little about to start a new life, possibly go to school, learn a trade, and become a good, loyal citizen. (Raymond Federman, *Double or Nothing*, c.1971.)

- High, high above the North Pole, on the first day of 1969, two professors of English Literature approached each other at a combined velocity of 1200 miles per hour. (David Lodge, *Changing Places*, c.1975.)

7. LET'S MEET JACK OR JILL

When the novel opens with a description of a character or explanation of a character's actions, it promises a character-centered story from the viewpoint of an omniscient and opinionated narrator. Unlike "set-up" this approach offers no particular narrative promise, only that it will be about this character. It often signals a morality tale or at least a cautionary lesson: there's no use in meeting Jack or Jill if there's not point to meeting him/her.

- Lolita, light of my life, fire of my loins. (Vladimir Nabokov, *Lolita*, c.1955.)
- Somewhere in la Mancha, in a place whose name I do not care to remember, a gentleman lived not long ago, one of those who has a lance and ancient shield on a shelf and keeps a skinny nag and a greyhound for racing. (Miguel de Cervantes (trans. Edith Grossman), *Don Quixote*, c.1605.)
- There was a boy called Eustace Clarence Scrubb, and he almost deserved it. (C. S. Lewis, *The Voyage of the Dawn Treader*, c.1952.)

- He was an old man who fished alone in a skiff in the Gulf Stream and he had gone eighty-four days now without taking a fish. (Ernest Hemingway, *The Old Man and the Sea*, c.1952.)
- Miss Brooke had that kind of beauty which seems to be thrown into relief by poor dress. (George Eliot, *Middlemarch*, c.1872.)
- What if this young woman, who writes such bad poems, in competition with her husband, whose poems are equally bad, should stretch her remarkably long and well-made legs out before you, so that her skirt slips up to the tops of her stockings? (Gilbert Sorrentino, *Imaginative Qualities of Actual Things*, c.1971.)
- When Dick Gibson was a little boy he was not Dick Gibson. (Stanley Elkin, *The Dick Gibson Show*, c.1971.)
- She waited, Kate Croy, for her father to come in, but he kept her unconscionably, and there were moments at which she showed herself, in the glass over the mantel, a face positively pale with the irritation that had brought her to the point of going away without sight of him. (Henry James, *The Wings of the Dove*, c.1902.)
- He was an inch, perhaps two, under six feet, powerfully built, and he advanced straight at you with a slight stoop of the shoulders, head forward, and a fixed from-under stare which made you think of a charging bull. (Joseph Conrad, *Lord Jim*, c.1900.)
- In the last years of the Seventeenth Century there was to be found among the fops and fools of the London coffee-houses one rangy, gangling flitch called Ebenezer Cooke, more ambitious than talented, and yet more talented than prudent, who, like his friends-in-folly, all of whom were supposed to be educating at Oxford or Cambridge, had

found the sound of Mother English more fun to game with than her sense to labor over, and so rather than applying himself to the pains of scholarship, had learned the knack of versifying, and ground out quires of couplets after the fashion of the day, afroth with Joves and Jupiters, aclang with jarring rhymes, and string-taut with similes stretched to the snapping-point. (John Barth, *The Sot-Weed Factor*, c.1960.)

- He was born with a gift of laughter and a sense that the world was mad. (Raphael Sabatini, *Scaramouche*, c.1921.)

8. "LET'S MEET JOE, MY FRIEND."

Opening a novel by introducing a friend makes it still observational, but from a first-person vantage. It has the advantage of telling the reader about both the narrator and the person described.

- Once upon a time, there was a woman who discovered she had turned into the wrong person. (Anne Tyler, *Back When We Were Grownups*, c.2001.)
- When I finally caught up with Abraham Trahearne, he was drinking beer with an alcoholic bulldog named Fireball Roberts in a ramshackle joint just outside of Sonoma, California, drinking the heart right out of a fine spring afternoon. (James Crumley, *The Last Good Kiss*, c.1978.)

9. I AM

This novel opening is a variation of meeting a character, except this time, the first-person narrator is giving a summary or a judgment about themselves. It's often a skewed perspective and should definitely introduce a great voice. This navel-gazing is so 21st century, don't you think?

- Call me Ishmael. (Herman Melville, *Moby-Dick*, c.1851.)

- I am an invisible man. (Ralph Ellison, *Invisible Man*, c.1952.)

- I am a sick man . . . I am a spiteful man. (Fyodor Dostoyevsky (trans. Michael R. Katz), *Notes from Underground*, c.1864.)

- In a sense, I am Jacob Horner. (John Barth, *The End of the Road*, c.1958.)

- I was born twice: first, as a baby girl, on a remarkably smogless Detroit day in January of 1960; and then again, as a teenage boy, in an emergency room near Petoskey, Michigan, in August of 1974. (Jeffrey Eugenides, *Middlesex*, c.2002.)

- If I am out of my mind, it's all right with me, thought Moses Herzog. (Saul Bellow, *Herzog*, c.1964.)

- Granted: I am an inmate of a mental hospital; my keeper is watching me, he never lets me out of his sight; there's a peephole in the door, and my keeper's eye is the shade of brown that can never see through a blue-eyed type like me. (Gynter Grass (trans. Ralph Manheim), *The Tin Drum*, c.1959.)

- I, Tiberius Claudius Drusus Nero Germanicus This-that-and-the-other (for I shall not trouble you yet with all my titles) who was once, and not so long ago either, known to my friends and relatives and associates as "Claudius the Idiot," or "That Claudius," or "Claudius the Stammerer," or "Clau-Clau-Claudius" or at best as "Poor Uncle Claudius," am now about to write this strange history of my life; starting from my earliest childhood and continuing year by year until I reach the fateful point of change where, some eight years ago, at the age of fifty-one, I suddenly found myself caught in what I may call the "golden predicament" from which I have never since become disentangled. (Robert Graves, *I, Claudius*, c.1934.)

- I am an American, Chicago born--Chicago, that somber city--and go at things as I have taught myself, free-style, and will make the record in my own way: first to knock, first admitted; sometimes an innocent knock, sometimes a not so innocent. (Saul Bellow, *The Adventures of Augie March*, c.1953.)

- I will tell you in a few words who I am: lover of the hummingbird that darts to the flower beyond the rotted sill where my feet are propped; lover of bright needlepoint and the bright stitching fingers of humorless old ladies bent to their sweet and infamous designs; lover of parasols made from the same puffy stuff as a young girl's underdrawers; still lover of that small naval boat which somehow survived the distressing years of my life between her decks or in her pilothouse; and also lover of poor dear black Sonny, my mess boy, fellow victim and confidant, and of my wife and child. But most of all, lover of my harmless and sanguine self. (John Hawkes, *Second Skin*, c.1964.)

10. MISLEADING LINES

Sometimes a novel begins with a line that is misleading, or with a line that needs the second, or succeeding lines, to get the full impact. There may be some openings that belong here, but an editor might not always read that second line.

- Mother died today. (Albert Camus (trans. Stuart Gilbert), *The Stranger*, c.1942.)

11. ALTERNATIVE MEDIA

Some stories rely on other forms to tell a story such as letters, diary, autobiography, schedules, official papers, etc. These documents or pseudo-documents give the author some authority. Some forms give opportunity for an intimate voice, such as diaries. This was one of Susan Lumenello's original categories, but I didn't find any that fit it in this list. It is still a valid way to open a story, of course, but it seems it's not very popular with literary critics.

12. SCREENPLAY (OR GRAPHIC NOVEL)

Likewise, this was another of Susan Lumenello's original categories, but I've not included examples. It starts a novel by using tag lines such as date, place, or time. It's a minimalist way to start a story, but it can establish immediacy and imprint the reader with a moment or image. Interestingly, as I looked at some graphic novels, this is the way some of them start.

CASE STUDY: TRYING 12 OPENING LINES

While working on rewriting the opening chapter of a novel, I decided to try the twelve strategies for opening a novel, post it on my blog (darcypattison.com) and request feedback. Here, then, are the twelve openings that follow the twelve strategies for opening lines. I asked my readers to comment on which one grabbed their attention and made them want to know more? I also asked for comments as to why it worked.

1. It was: It was a brisk spring morning, the day that Laurel and her Father went to inspect Sloth.
2. Viewpoint on life: Cathedrals take time to build, sometimes decades; and as the walls grow, people come and go, live and die. So it was that Laurel came one day with her Father to inspect Sloth.

3. Mid-action: Laurel groped for Sloth's cold cheek and caressed the rough stone.

4. Dialogue: "Has Sloth survived this bitter winter?"

5. Landscape: From her perch atop a twenty-foot ladder, Laurel looked across the rooftops of St. Stephens Cathedral at the graceful lines of the stone building and the gargoyles that capped every gutter.

6. Landscape alternate: The city of Montague lay quiet on this early spring morning, except for a brisk wind romping about amidst the towers and gargoyles of the Cathedral of St. Stephens.

7. SetUp: When Laurel turned up missing, her father and the priests of the Cathedral of St. Stephens lit candles in prayer and searched and pleaded with the heavens for news of her, but they didn't think to look up. It began on a spring day...

8. Meet Jack or Jill: Laurel was tiny, like a hummingbird, her Father said.

9. Let's meet Joe, My Friend: If Laurel was a friend to all gargoyles, her Father was the god of the gargoyles, the master creator.

10. I am: I am frozen in time, a girl who cannot move forward or backward.

11. Misleading lines: I hate cathedrals, all that stone surrounding a person is creepy.

12. Alternative media:
    To: All Priests of the River Province
    From: Cardinal Pater
    We beseech you, brethren, to be on the lookout for a missing girl, one Laurel Raymond, daughter of Master Raymond, architect of the Cathedral of St. Stephens.

13. Screenplay:

Date: Two weeks after the spring solstice

Where: City of Montague, home of the Cathedral of St. Stephens

Openings: And the Winner Is...

I am always amazed anew at how much a reader can infer from just an opening sentence. My blog readers inferred setting, time of year, approximate century, the main conflict of the story, and much more.

The comments on these openings fell into three camps. There are those who love to read a good first-person narrative. These folks voted for this version:

> *"I am frozen in time, a girl who cannot move forward or backward."*

Some readers love history and historical fiction. These people generally liked the landscape or viewpoint on life (One person commented, "You had me at 'cathedrals'."):

> *Cathedrals take time to build, sometimes decades; and as the walls grow, people come and go, live and die. So it was that Laurel came one day with her Father to inspect Sloth.*

> OR:

> *From her perch atop a twenty-foot ladder, Laurel looked across the rooftops of St. Stephens Cathedral at the graceful lines of the stone building and the gargoyles which capped every gutter.*

There are those who just like to know where a story is going. These folks were the overwhelming winners by choosing the set-up:

When Laurel turned up missing, her father and the priests of the Cathedral of St. Stephens lit candles in prayer and searched and pleaded with the heavens for news of her, but they didn't think to look up. It began on a spring day...

MY REACTION TO FEEDBACK

Surprise. I am always surprised by feedback. If I had thought readers would think about my story THAT way, I would have written slightly different. My vision is rarely crystal clear on the pages of a first draft and feedback lets me see where the story on paper has gaping holes.

In this case, I was surprised that the Set Up version worked best.

One commenter said, "...I myself start stories for Middle Grade readers mid-action, because I think that age group responds best to short, emphatic sentences & paragraphs filled with action (as opposed to rumination)..."

I agree that novels or stories meant for kids should begin in an exciting way. The Set Up version is a long sentence and doesn't begin in the middle of the action; I had to add on the "It began on a spring day..." It doesn't seem the right sort of opening for the audience.

Audience does matter. For adults, you might get away with a different strategy for starting a story. And here's the problem with feedback. My blog readers are adults; did the commenters respond as adults, or did they try to put themselves in the shoes of middle grade readers? I don't know. All I know is the Set Up version was popular.

I was also surprised that Set Up was chosen by most because, for me, it gives away the ending. I wondered if there was a way to signal the ending better—to foreshadow it, without giving it away totally. Certainly, it would be pages and pages before a reader would know what I meant by that Set Up; and if it gets the reader to the next sentence, to turn the page, maybe it is better.

What is the goal of an opening sentence? To pull you forward to read the next sentence. Period.

Try a variety of first lines, and then move on. You'll have a chance to revise it later.

Notes

[1] Lumenello, Susan. "The Promise of the First Line," *The Writer's Chronicle*, Volume 38, Number 3, December 2005.

[2] http://americanbookreview.org/100BestLines.asp

[7]

STEP FIVE: Now, Write!

In fiction, a valuable idea is that of a placeholder. That is, you write something–a sentence, a title, a paragraph, a joke, a piece of dialogue–knowing that this isn't the best it can be, but also knowing that you'll come back and fix it. This bit of writing is just "holding the place" until you get time to choose the perfect words.

Placeholders have an important function in the first draft. They let you get the story told without fussing over the exact details. You get a sense of momentum, that you are moving forward. The story is the focus of the first draft, getting it down on paper, from first to last, opening scene to climax to denouement.

The function of the first draft is to find your story.

The function of the next few drafts is to find the best way to tell that story.

While we are saying that the opening line, paragraph, scene and chapter are extremely important, in the end, you must just write. Use placeholders when you're not sure what to write, and know that you'll be back. Placeholders in a first draft make perfect sense.

Your job now it to take your opening line and expand it to a paragraph, a scene, a chapter, Act 1 and then move on to the rest of the story. Go on! Start your story!

[8]

STEP SIX: Revise

Once you have a full draft of a novel written, it's time to go back and evaluate, time to fix all those placeholders. My workbook, *Novel Metamorphosis: Uncommon Ways to Revise*, discusses the full novel revision in detail. Here, we will talk about revising the opening.

I am sometimes asked to read a novel for someone and I've learned that there are specific things that make me stop reading:

NOTHING HAPPENED. The whole first chapter could be cut, because no major action occurred. Ask yourself: what happened in this chapter? Is there any conflict here?

THE VOICE WAS FLAT, MONOTONE AND UNINTERESTING. Read it aloud: Does the text demand that you use an interesting variation of pitches, tones, stops, starts, etc? Does it have an appealing voice?

INCONSISTENCIES. If I found myself thinking, "No, that couldn't happen, not that way," then the story was in trouble. Consider: does the story's logic work?

BACKSTORY. Let me repeat: don't put backstory in the first chapter. Give readers an active scene with the character in motion and wanting something. It doesn't have to be the major goal of the book, but the character needs to want something and it should be something that leads into the main conflict. Ask yourself: Do I really need to explain the backstory here, or can I wait until page 100? Yes! Page 100! Move that boring stuff out of the first act entirely!

THE POINT-OF-VIEW JUMPS OUT AT ME. Too often manuscripts have first-person point-of-views that jump out and make me cringe. In other words, the voice isn't distinctive enough for first person. The default point-of-view should be third-person unless there is a compelling reason for first. It's not just a bias against first-person, but rather, that the story would be better served from third in many cases.

I've read some first-person novels where I didn't even realize it because the story caught me. When it works, it works well. When it fails, the story might be salvaged by a switch to third. Consider: Is there a compelling reason for the first-person point-of-view? Could this ONLY be told from first? Try–OK, just try–writing the first chapter from third and give it to an independent, unbiased reader and ask which version they like better. Don't tell them what the difference is—just ask which version they like better.

When you revise your novel or story do you look at what you wrote before or start totally from scratch? Young Adult author Cynthia Leitich Smith says, "Back when every novel I wrote was wholly new, I used to write a 'discovery draft' wherein, after some prewriting, I plunged in and wrote a full story (with a beginning, middle, and end—say, 35,000 to 60,000 words) to get to know my protagonists, their goals and their world. When I was done, I would print it. Read it. Toss it. And delete the file. It sounds harsh, I know. But the idea was to take some of the pressure off. Nobody but me would ever read that dreaded first draft. And I certainly wasn't planning to build on such a shaky foundation."

For another interesting story of writing exploratory drafts, read Amy Tan's discussion of writing her second novel—the all important sophomore novel—after her successful first novel, *The Joy Luck Club*. In her memoir, *The Opposite of Fate: Memories of a Writing Life*, Tan details her long, but eventually successful process.

The first draft of a story is to tell you what the story is. The next drafts are a search for the best way to tell this story. They are different processes with different purposes.

Unlike Smith, I work with the text I already have written. The idea here is that I'm close, but it isn't quite there yet. In this case, I'm refining the text and story as I go. The story gets minor improvements in specificity with more Show-don't-Tell sensory details. Or, the pace is quickened or varied more. The text itself is revised to eliminate extraneous words, while listening carefully for the rhythms of the paragraphs, the exactness of word choice—in short, for voice.

I may also delete chapters, add chapters or move chapters around, working to tighten the tension of the plot. Nothing is safe from being deleted or changed when doing this draft. It is a honing of the story written in the first draft.

WHY SHOULD THE READER CARE?

A book that helps you think about the revisions needed in the opening is *Reading Like a Writer*, by Francine Prose. She encourages writers to consider the appropriateness of each and every word. With a class, she'll often read a novel's opening and the class considers alternatives to almost every word.

Taking a page from her, here are a couple openings from a works-in-progress.

"Eliot Winston! Come here."

> *That Mrs. Lopez, her voice cut through even the jumpy music from the loud-speakers. I was sure her voice could cut through anything, even concrete. "Yes, ma'am," I said and steered Marj toward The Voice.*

In this opening, we know there is a first person POV main character. We assume that Mrs. Lopez is also a main character (incorrect: she's only a supporting character). We're in a place with loud music and there's another character named Marj there, but we have no idea who she is. From the sentence construction (That Mrs. Lopez, her voice. . .), we get a touch of the character's voice and understand that maybe he's jumpy. Jumpy, concrete–these two words are perhaps setting up the emotional context of the story.

The main problem with this opening is that Mrs. Lopez is highlighted too much, and it's unclear where we are. It's confusing with three characters introduced so rapidly. Where should the reader focus? In spite of the demanding tone of Mrs. Lopez and the questions raised, mostly, the reader is confused.

> *Ba-boom, ba-boom, ba-boom.*
>
> *Standing outside the gymnasium doors, a drum beat throbbed. Yellow light streamed from the second story windows, the ones Toby and I looked out of when we sat at the top of the bleachers. I couldn't hear the music's melody, just the drum beat: ba-boom, ba-boom.*
>
> *The Back-to-School party at Wilma Rudolph Elementary School had already started.*

In this revised opening, tension is set up right away with the drumbeats; perhaps the character's heart is also beating hard, an implication that certainly works. It's very clear that we are outside a gymnasium at a back-to-school party. There's a sense of anticipation, of wanting to know what will happen when this character steps into the gymnasium and this party.

It's a quieter opening in some ways, but the anticipation of entering the party will carry the reader a few more paragraphs. So, I have those paragraphs to make the reader CARE about what will happen.

Toby is mentioned now, and he's the character's best friend. It's better to introduce him indirectly at the beginning than to introduce Mrs. Lopez.

Where Does the Engine Start?

Sol Stein, in *Stein on Writing* has another hint at what works in writing openings to novels. He asks, "Where does the engine get started?" By this he means where does the reader's interest sit up and take notice, the point at which "the reader decides not to put the book down." And often, it's with a single word or phrase.

> *On Friday noon, July the twentieth, 1714, the finest bridge in all Peru broke and precipitated five travelers into the gulf below. –opening of* The Bridge of San Luis Rey *by Thornton Wilder.*

Wow, what a lot gets accomplished in this snippet! Time, location and conflict. It's the contrast between two words, "finest" bridge and "broke" that catches my interest. Why did the finest bridge break?

Where exactly does the engine start in your novel? Locate it and underline it. If it's not on the first page, can you cut everything before it? Or, can you move it to the first page?

The Page 5 Test

I also like to check how well I am doing on characterization, one of the most important aspects of the novel's opening. Here's how I do it.

Read the first five pages of your manuscript (typed, double-spaced, standard formatting).

Turn over page 5 and on the back, write everything you know about the main character from those first 5 pages.

Things to record: name, age, location, family role and family details, likes, dislikes, fears, passions, ways of speaking, verbal tics, physical characteristics and tics.

No fair cheating and adding things that you know about the character, but you didn't put on the page.

No fair looking back; the characterization must be sharp enough that the character starts to come to life and your reader doesn't have to look up details.

Stop! Go do the Page 5 Test on your WIP Right NOW. Then come back.

CHARACTERIZATION: STRONG OR WEAK?

Now it's time to evaluate how well you did. Here are some things the Page 5 Test might reveal.

LACK OF INFORMATION. Often basic information is missing in the first five pages. In a first person POV novel, the character's name may not be clear until way after page 5. Yes, the point-of-view is in the character's head and it's hard to work in the name. Please don't resort to a clichéd way of working in a person's name: she absently writes it on a piece of paper, she talks to herself by name, etc. Somehow, though, I want to know the character's name, please. At least by the end of page 5.

BORING. The character's voice, whether the story is first or third, is clichéd and boring. Well, it's hard to be honest about this! If you find you can't be honest, hand the story to a friend or colleague. Lie, and tell them that this is a manuscript you're reading for a friend; or tell them it's a manuscript by whatever famous author you'd like to emulate. Ask your reader: after page 5, would you keep reading? Why or why not?

SHALLOW. Often, we know the character's name, maybe their age, one or two things about the family, their physical appearance (often in great detail) and. . .well, not much more. The characterization is shallow. We get a cartoon character like Betty Boop or Wile E. Coyote. We don't know or care about this character yet. That translates into a reader shutting the book and not reading further.

By page 5, good characterization will be a list of 8-10 things about the character and a voice that keeps the reader turning the page.

Celebrate the Good, Fix the Needy Characterization

Not to worry. We all know that first drafts—and sometimes even 8th drafts—are just unspeakably bad. But that's what the next draft is for.

First, NOTICE WHAT YOU DID WELL! I put that in caps because otherwise, you'll be like me and skip the good parts. You did something well. Notice this! Celebrate your Bright Spots.

But, also realize you have room for improvement. In the next draft, maybe you need to work on:

VOICE. You may actually know this character inside and out, but just didn't capture that on the page. In that case, you'll need to experiment with voice for the character and narrative voice for your story.

PLOT. While you're doing experimenting for voice, you may need to try three or four different opening scenes until you find one that allows for a rich development of both plot and character. Remember, we don't need to have all the backstory up front; we don't need to have all the character questions answered. What we need is to be intrigued by this person and want to know more. That's why we read on.

CHARACTER. Most people read a novel or story to become acquainted with people. Grab them up front with a great character and you'll keep the reader for the long haul.

THE BEGINNING COMES LAST?

National Book Award winner and Young Adult author, Richard Peck has this working method:

> *"When I finish the book, I take the first chapter and, without rereading it, throw it away. Then I write the first chapter last, now that I know how the story ends. It means I write the first chapter with confidence because the first chapter is the last chapter in disguise." --Richard Peck, "A Conversation with Richard Peck," in his book Fair Weather, Puffin Books edition, 2001.*

By the time you finish writing a whole novel, it's often true that the opening that pleased you so much at the beginning is no longer appropriate. Sometimes, you need to write or rewrite extensively the opening that matches what the novel has become.

It matters little if you keep the original chapter or if you rewrite it totally in the revisions. What matters is that the original chapter pulled you along to the next chapter and the next. What does matter is that the manuscript you send to an editor has a compelling first line, paragraph, scene and chapter. What matters is that the published novel grabs the reader. at the first word and never lets go.

Index

ABOUT THE AUTHOR

Author, blogger, and writing teacher Darcy Pattison (www.darcypattison.com) has been published in eight languages. Recent nature books for children include: *WISDOM, THE MIDWAY ALBATROSS*, which earned a Starred Review in *Publisher's Weekly*; *DESERT BATHS*, an NSTA Outstanding Science Trade Book 2013, and *PRAIRIE STORMS*. Her picture book *THE JOURNEY OF OLIVER K. WOODMAN* (Harcourt) was starred by BCCB and Kirkus, and was an Irma Simonton Black and James H. Black Award for Excellence in Children's Literature Honor book and is included in an HMH reading textbook. She travels the U. S. teaching a novel revision retreat using her workbook, *NOVEL METAMORPHOSIS: Uncommon Ways to Revise*. Other ebooks for writers include *How to Write a Children's Picture Book*, and *The Book Trailer Manual*. Darcy Pattison is the 2007 recipient of Arkansas Governor's Arts Awards for her work in Children's Literature.

Made in the USA
San Bernardino, CA
06 June 2014